IN THE BLINK OF AN EYE

IN THE BLINK OF AN EYE

A PERSPECTIVE ON FILM EDITING

WALTER MURCH

SILMAN-JAMES PRESS
Los Angeles

First Edition
10 9 8 7 6 5

Permission was graciously extended by the respective publishers for the use of material from the following works:

The Magic Lantern by Ingmar Bergman, p. 35. © 1988 Viking Press, New York, NY, 10010. Translation by Joan Tate. Originally published as *Lanterna Magica* in 1987 by Norstedts Forlag, Sweden. Reproduced by permission of Hamish Hamilton Ltd., London.

Language in Four Dimensions by William Stokoe. New York Academy of Sciences, 1979.

Christian Science Monitor, interview with John Huston by staff writer Louise Sweeney, August 11, 1973.

Photos from the film *The Unbearable Lightness of Being* used with permission of the Saul Zaentz Co. All rights reserved. © 1988

Library of Congress Cataloging-in-Publication Data

Murch, Walter, 1943-
In the blink of an eye : a perspective on film editing / by Walter Murch
p. cm.
1. Motion pictures—Editing.   I. Title.
TR899.M87   1995   778.5'35--dc20   95-44984
ISBN: 1-879505-23-1

Cover design by Heidi Frieder
Cover photographs by Michael D. Brown
Printed and bound in the United States of America

Silman-James Press
1181 Angelo Drive
Beverly Hills, CA 90210

This is a revised transcription of a lecture on film editing given by Walter Murch in the mixing theater at Spectrum Films, Sydney, Australia, in October 1988. It was one in a series of lectures sponsored by the Australian Film Commission.

Sections of this lecture were also included in a presentation given in February 1990 to the Advanced Editing class taught by Barbara and Richard Marks as part of the UCLA Graduate School of Theater, Film, and Television.

In 1995, the main text of this book was revised and the Afterword was written to supplement and expand some of the thoughts contained in the lecture.

Contents

Foreword

*T*he thought of Walter Murch brings a smile to my face. I'm not sure exactly why. It must be the combination of his unique personality, the security inspired by his competence, and his gentleness and wisdom. Gerald MacBoingBoing grown up, still playful and enigmatic, but grounded by an immense intelligence.

Perhaps it's also because he was the essential collaborator on what are probably the best films I worked on: *The Conversation* and *The Godfather Part II.* I have a very soft spot in my heart for those films, and *The Rain People,* because only they were the closest to the goal I had set for myself as a young man: to write original stories and screenplays only. This is something Walter always encouraged me to do, and was best achieved working with him. But Walter is a study unto himself: a philosopher and theoretician of film—a gifted director in his own right, attested to by his beautiful *Return to Oz.* Nothing is so fascinating as spending hours listening to Walter's theories of life, cinema, and the countless tidbits of wisdom that he leaves behind him like Hansel and Gretel's trail of bread: guidance and nourishment.

I smile also because we are so different from one another: Whereas I make instantaneous decisions relying on emotion and intuition only, Walter is *also* thoughtful and careful and methodical in every step he takes. Whereas I alternate between the ecstatic and despondent like Tesla's alternating current, Walter is constant and warm and reassuring. Every bit as ingenious and intuitive as I am, he is also constant.

Walter is a pioneer, as I would like to be, and the kind of person who should be listened to carefully and enjoyed. For all this, I imagine you would think that I love and respect Walter Murch very much—and I certainly do.

Francis Coppola
Napa, 1995

Preface

Igor Stravinsky loved expressing himself and wrote a
good deal on interpretation. As he bore a volcano
within him, he urged restraint. Those without even
the vestige of a volcano within them nodded in
agreement, raised their baton, and observed restraint,
while Stravinsky himself conducted his own *Apollon
Musagète* as if it were Tchaikovsky. We who had
read him listened and were astonished.

The Magic Lantern by Ingmar Bergman

*M*ost of us are searching—consciously or unconsciously—for a degree of internal balance and
harmony between ourselves and the outside world,
and if we happen to become aware—like Stravinsky—
of a volcano within us, we will compensate by urging
restraint. By the same token, someone who bore a
glacier within him might urge passionate abandon. The
danger is, as Bergman points out, that a glacial personality in need of passionate abandon may read
Stravinsky and apply restraint instead.

Many of the thoughts that follow, although presented to the public in a lecture, are therefore more truly cautionary notes to myself, working methods I have developed for coping with my own particular volcanoes and glaciers. As such, they are insights into one person's search for balance, and are perhaps interesting to others more for the glimpses of the search itself than for the specific methods that search has produced.

I would like to thank Ken Sallows for providing me with the transcription of the original lecture and the opportunity to present it to a wider audience. For cosmetic reasons, I have made certain revisions and added some footnotes to what was, for the most part, an extemporaneous dialogue between myself and the audience, whom I thank for their interest and participation. I have also updated some technical points and added an afterword that considers the impact that nonlinear, digital editing has had on the process of filmmaking.

Special thanks also to Hilary Furlong (then of the Australian Film Commission), who was instrumental in bringing me to Australia, where the lecture was originally given.

Walter Murch
Rome, August 1995

Cuts and Shadow Cuts

*I*t is frequently at the edges of things that we learn most about the middle: ice and steam can reveal more about the nature of water than water alone ever could. While it is true that any film worth making is going to be unique, and the conditions under which films are made are so variable that it is misleading to speak about what is "normal," *Apocalypse Now,* by almost any criteria—schedule, budget, artistic ambition, technical innovation—qualifies as the cinematic equivalent of ice and steam. Just considering the length of time it took to complete the film (I was editing picture for one year and spent another year preparing and mixing the sound), it turned out to be the longest post-production of any picture I have worked on, but that may consequently spill some light on what "normal" is, or might be.[1]

One of the reasons for that length was simply the amount of film that had been printed: 1,250,000 feet,

---

[1] And I had come on relatively late in the process. Richie Marks and Jerry Greenberg had already been editing for nine months when I joined them in August 1977, a few months after the end of shooting, and the three of us worked together until Jerry left in the spring of 1978. Richie and I then continued together, joined by Lisa Fruchtman, until I began to work on the soundtrack.

which works out to be just over 230 hours. Since the finished film runs just under two hours and twenty-five minutes in length, that gives a ratio of ninety-five to one. That is to say, ninety-five "unseen" minutes for every minute that found its way into the finished product. By comparison, the average ratio for theatrical features is around twenty to one.

Traveling across that ninety-five-to-one landscape was a little like forging through a thick forest, bursting upon open grassland for a while, then plunging into a forest again because there were areas, such as the helicopter sequences, where the coverage was extremely high, and other scenes where the coverage was correspondingly low. I think the Colonel Kilgore scenes alone were over 220,000 feet—and since that represents twenty-five minutes of film in the finished product, the ratio there was around one hundred to one. But many of the connecting scenes had only a master shot: Francis had used so much film and time on the big events that he compensated with minimal coverage on some of these linking scenes.

Take one of the big scenes as an example: The helicopter attack on "Charlie's Point," where Wagner's *Ride of the Valkyries* is played, was staged as an actual event and consequently filmed as a documentary rather than a series of specially composed shots. It was choreography on a vast scale of men, machines, cameras, and landscape—like some kind of diabolical toy that you could wind up and then let go. Once Francis said, "Action," the filming resembled actual combat: Eight cameras turning simultaneously (some on the ground and some in helicopters) each loaded with a thousand-foot (eleven-minute) roll of film.

At the end of one of these shots, unless there had been an obvious problem, the camera positions were changed and the whole thing was repeated. Then repeated again, and then again. They kept on going until, I guess, they felt that they had enough material, each take generating something like 8,000 feet (an hour and a half). No single take was the same as any other—very much like documentary coverage.

Anyway, at the end of it all, when the film was safely in the theaters, I sat down and figured out the total number of days that we (the editors) had worked, divided that number by the number of cuts that were in the finished product, and came up with the rate of cuts per editor per day—which turned out to be . . . 1.47!

Meaning that, if we had somehow known *exactly* where we were going at the beginning, we would have arrived there in the same number of months if each of us had made just under one-and-a-half splices per day. In other words, if I had sat down at my bench in the morning, made one cut, thought about the next cut, and gone home, then come in the next day, made the cut I thought about the day before, made another cut, and gone home, it would have taken me the same year it actually took to edit my sections of the film.

Since it takes under ten seconds to make one-and-a-half splices, the admittedly special case of *Apocalypse Now* serves to throw into exaggerated relief the fact that editing—even on a "normal" film[2]—is not so

---

[2] By comparison, an average theatrical feature might have a cuts-per-day figure of eight.

much a *putting together* as it is a *discovery of a path,* and that the overwhelming majority of an editor's time is not spent actually splicing film. The more film there is to work with, of course, the greater the number of pathways that can be considered, and the possibilities compound upon each other and consequently demand more time for evaluation. This is true for any film with a high shooting ratio, but in the particular case of *Apocalypse* the effect was magnified by a sensitive subject matter and a daring and unusual structure, technical innovations at every level, and the obligation felt by all concerned to do the very best work they were capable of. And perhaps most of all by the fact that this was, for Francis, a personal film, despite the large budget and the vast canvas of the subject. Regrettably few films combine such qualities and aspirations.

For every splice in the finished film there were probably fifteen "shadow" splices—splices made, considered, and then undone or lifted from the film. But even allowing for that, the remaining eleven hours and fifty-eight minutes of each working day were spent in activities that, in their various ways, served to clear and illuminate the path ahead of us: screenings, discussions, rewinding, re-screenings, meetings, scheduling, filing trims, note-taking, bookkeeping, and lots of plain deliberative thought. A vast amount of preparation, really, to arrive at the innocuously brief moment of decisive action: the cut—the moment of transition from one shot to the next—something that, appropriately enough, should look almost self-evidently simple and effortless, if it is even noticed at all.

Why Do Cuts Work?

*W*ell, the fact is that *Apocalypse Now*, as well as every other theatrical film (except perhaps Hitchcock's *Rope*[3]), is made up of many different pieces of film joined together into a mosaic of images. The mysterious part of it, though, is that the joining of those pieces—the "cut" in American terminology[4]—actually does seem to work, even though it represents a total and instantaneous displacement of one field of vision with another, a displacement that sometimes also entails a jump forward or backward in time as well as space.

It works; but it could easily have been otherwise, since nothing in our day-to-day experience seems to prepare us for such a thing. Instead, from the moment we get up in the morning until we close our eyes at night, the visual reality we perceive is a continuous

---

[3] A film composed of only ten shots, each ten minutes long, invisibly joined together, so that the impression is of a complete lack of editing.

[4] I was aware, talking to an Australian audience, of the bias inherent in our respective languages. In the States, film is "cut," which puts the emphasis on *separation*. In Australia (and in Great Britain), film is "joined," with the emphasis on *bringing together*.

stream of linked images: In fact, for millions of years—tens, hundreds of millions of years—life on Earth has experienced the world this way. Then suddenly, at the beginning of the twentieth century, human beings were confronted with something else—edited film.

Under these circumstances, it wouldn't have been at all surprising to find that our brains had been "wired" by evolution and experience to reject film editing. If that had been the case, then the single-shot movies of the Lumière Brothers—or films like Hitchcock's *Rope*—would have become the standard. For a number of practical (as well as artistic) reasons, it is good that it did not.

The truth of the matter is that film is actually being "cut" twenty-four times a second. Each frame is a displacement from the previous one—it is just that in a continuous shot, the space/time displacement from frame to frame is small enough (twenty milliseconds) for the audience to see it as *motion within a context* rather than as twenty-four different contexts a second. On the other hand, when the visual displacement is great enough (as at the moment of the cut), we are forced to re-evaluate the new image as a *different context*: miraculously, most of the time we have no problem in doing this.

What we *do* seem to have difficulty accepting are the kind of displacements that are neither subtle nor total: Cutting from a full-figure master shot, for instance, to a slightly tighter shot that frames the actors from the ankles up. The new shot in this case is different enough to signal that *something* has changed, but not different enough to make us re-evaluate its context: The displacement of the image is neither motion nor change of context, and the collision of these two ideas produces a mental jarring—a jump— that is comparatively disturbing.[5]

At any rate, the discovery early in this century that certain kinds of cutting "worked" led almost immediately to the discovery that films could be shot discontinuously, which was the cinematic equivalent of the discovery of flight: In a practical sense, films were no longer "earthbound" in time and space. If we could make films only by assembling all the elements simultaneously, as in the theater, the range of possible subjects would be comparatively narrow. Instead, Discontinuity is King: It is the central fact during the production phase of filmmaking, and almost all decisions are directly related to it in one way or another— how to overcome its difficulties and/or how to best take advantage of its strengths.[6]

The other consideration is that even if everything *were* available simultaneously, it is just very difficult

---

[5] A beehive can apparently be moved two inches each night without disorienting the bees the next morning. Surprisingly, if it is moved two *miles,* the bees also have no problem: They are forced by the total displacement of their environment to re-orient their sense of direction, which they can do easily enough. But if the hive is moved two *yards,* the bees will become fatally confused. The environment does not seem different to them, so they do not re-orient themselves, and as a result, they will not recognize their own hive when they return from foraging, hovering instead in the empty space where the hive used to be, while the hive itself sits just two yards away.

[6] When Stanley Kubrick was directing *The Shining*, he wanted to shoot the film in continuity and to have all sets and actors available all the time. He took over almost the entire studio at Elstree (London), built all the sets simultaneously, and they sat there, pre-lit, for however long it took him to shoot the film. But *The Shining* remains a special exception to the general rule of discontinuity.

to shoot long, continuous takes and have all the contributing elements work each time. European filmmakers tend to shoot more complex master shots than the Americans, but even if you are Ingmar Bergman, there's a limit to what you can handle: Right at the end, some special effect might not work or someone might forget their lines or some lamp might blow a fuse, and now the whole thing has to be done again. The longer the take, of course, the greater the chances of a mistake.

So there is a considerable logistical problem of getting everything together at the same time, and then just as serious a problem in getting it all to "work" every time. The result is that, for practical reasons alone, we don't follow the pattern of the Lumière Brothers or of *Rope*.

On the other hand, apart from matters of convenience, discontinuity also allows us to choose the best camera angle for each emotion and story point, which we can edit together for a cumulatively greater impact. If we were limited to a continuous stream of images, this would be difficult, and films would not be as sharp and to the point as they are.[7]

---

[7] Visual discontinuity—although not in the temporal sense—is the most striking feature of Ancient Egyptian painting. Each part of the human body was represented by its most characteristic and revealing angle: head in profile, shoulders frontal, arms and legs in profile, torso frontal—and then all these different angles were combined in one figure. To us today, with our preference for the unifying laws of perspective, this gives an almost comic "twisted" look to the people of Ancient Egypt—but it may be that in some remote future, our films, with their combination of many different angles (each being the most "revealing" for its particular subject), will look just as comic and twisted.

And yet, beyond even these considerations, cutting is more than just the convenient means by which discontinuity is rendered continuous. It is in *and for itself*—by the very force of its paradoxical suddenness—a positive influence in the creation of a film. We would want to cut even if discontinuity were not of such great practical value.

So the central fact of all this is that cuts *do work*. But the question still remains: *Why?* It is kind of like the bumble-bee, which should not be able to fly, but does.

We will get back to this mystery in a few moments.

"Cut Out the Bad Bits"

*M*any years ago, my wife, Aggie, and I went back to England for our first anniversary (she is English, although we'd been married in the United States), and I met some of her childhood friends for the first time.

"Well, what is it that you do?" one of them asked, and I replied that I was studying film editing. "Oh, editing," he said, "that's where you cut out the bad bits." Of course, I became (politely) incensed: "It is much more than that. Editing is structure, color, dynamics, manipulation of time, all of these other things, etc., etc." What he had in mind was home movies: "Oop, there's a bad bit, cut it out and paste the rest back together." Actually, twenty-five years down the road, I've come to respect his unwitting wisdom.

Because, in a certain sense, editing *is* cutting out the bad bits, the tough question is, *What makes a bad bit?* When you are shooting a home movie and the camera wanders, that's obviously a bad bit, and it's clear that you want to cut it out. The goal of a home movie is usually pretty simple: an unrestructured record of events in continuous time. The goal of narrative films is much more complicated because of the fragmented time structure and the need to indicate internal states of being, and so it becomes proportionately more complicated to identify what is a "bad bit." And what is bad in one film may be good in another. In fact, one way of looking at the process of making a film is to think of it as the search to identify what—for the particular film you are working on—is a uniquely "bad bit." So, the editor embarks on the search to identify these "bad bits" and cut them out, provided that doing so does not disrupt the structure of the "good bits" that are left.

Which leads me to chimpanzees.

About forty years ago, after the double-helix structure of DNA was discovered, biologists hoped that they now had a kind of map of the genetic architecture of each organism. Of course, they didn't expect the structure of the DNA to look like the organism they were studying (the way a map of England *looks* like England), but rather that each point in the organism would somehow correspond to an equivalent point in the DNA.

That's not what they found, though. For instance, when they began to compare them closely, they were surprised to discover that the DNA for the human and the chimpanzee were surprisingly similar. So much so—ninety-nine percent identical—as to be inadequate to explain all of the obvious differences between us.

So where do the differences come from?

Biologists were eventually forced to realize that there must be something else—still under much discussion—that controlled the *order* in which the various pieces of information stored in the DNA would be activated and the *rates* at which that information would be activated as the organism grew.

In the early stages of fetal development, it is difficult to tell the difference between human and chimp embryos. And yet, as they grow, they reach a point where differences become apparent, and from that point on, the differences become more and more obvious. For instance, the choice of what comes first, the brain or the skull. In human beings, the priority is brain first, skull next, because the emphasis is on maximizing the size of the brain. Any time you look at a newborn human infant you can see that the skull is not yet fully closed around the top of the still-growing brain.

With chimpanzees, the priority is reversed: skull first, *then* brain—probably for reasons that have to do with the harsher environment into which the chimp is born. The command from the chimp's sequence is, "Fill up this empty space with as much brain as you can." But there's only so much brain you can get in there before you can't fill it up anymore. At any rate, it seems to be more important for a chimp to be born with a hard head than a big brain. There's a similar interplay between an endless list of things: The thumb and the fingers, skeletal posture, certain bones being fully formed before certain muscular developments, etc.

My point is that the information in the DNA can be seen as uncut film and the mysterious sequencing code as the editor. You could sit in one room with a pile of dailies and another editor could sit in the next room with exactly the same footage and both of you would make different films out of the same material. Each is going to make different choices about how to structure it, which is to say *when* and *in what order* to release those various pieces of information. Do we know, for instance, that the gun is loaded *before* Madame X gets into her car, or is that something we only learn *after* she is in the car? Either choice creates a different sense of the scene. And so you proceed, piling one difference on top of another. Reversing the comparison, you can look at the human and the chimp as different films edited from the same set of dailies.[8]

I'm not assigning relative values here to a chimpanzee or a human being. Let's just say that each is appropriate to the environment in which it belongs: I would be wrong swinging from a branch in the middle of the jungle, and a chimpanzee would be wrong writing this book. The point is not their intrinsic value, but rather the inadvisability of changing one's mind in the process of creating one of them. Don't start making a chimpanzee and then decide to turn it into a human being instead. That produces a stitched-together Frankenstein's monster, and we've all seen its equivalent in the theaters: Film "X" would have been a nice little movie, perfectly suited to its "environment," but in the middle of production someone got an inflated idea about its possibilities, and, as a result, it became boring and pretentious. It was

---

[8] By the same token, a chimpanzee and a cockroach are made from different "dailies" to begin with.

a chimpanzee film that someone tried to turn into a human-being film, and it came out being neither.

Or film "Y," which was an ambitious project that tried to deal with complex, subtle issues, but the studio got to it and ordered additional material to be shot, filled with action and sex, and, as a result, a great potential was reduced to something less, neither human nor chimp.

Most with the Least

*Y*ou can never judge the quality of a sound mix simply by counting the number of tracks it took to produce it. Terrible mixes have been produced from a hundred tracks. By the same token, wonderful mixes have been made from only three tracks. It depends on the initial choices that were made, the quality of the sounds, and how capable the blend of those sounds was of exciting emotions hidden in the hearts of the audience. The underlying principle: Always try to do the most with the least—with the emphasis on try. You may not always succeed, but *attempt* to produce the greatest effect in the viewer's mind by the least number of things on screen. Why? Because you want to do only what is necessary to engage the imagination of the audience—suggestion is always more effective than exposition. Past a certain point, the more effort you put into wealth of detail, the more you encourage the audience to become spectators rather than participants. The same principle applies to all the various crafts of filmmaking: acting, art direction, photography, music, costume, etc.

And, of course, it applies to editing as well. You would never say that a certain film was well-edited because it had more cuts in it. Frequently, it takes more work and discernment to decide where *not* to cut—don't feel you have to cut just because you are being paid to. You are being paid to make decisions, and as far as whether to cut or not, the editor is actually making twenty-four decisions a second: "No. No. No. No. No. No. No. No. No. No. Yes!"

An overactive editor, who changes shots too frequently, is like a tour guide who can't stop pointing things out: "And up there we have the Sistine Ceiling, and over here we have the Mona Lisa, and, by the way, look at these floor tiles . . ." If you are on a tour, you do want the guide to point things out for you, of course, but some of the time you just want to walk around and see what *you* see. If the guide—that is to say, the editor—doesn't have the confidence to let people themselves occasionally choose what they want to look at, or to leave things to their imagination, then he is pursuing a goal (complete control) that in the end is self-defeating. People will eventually feel constrained and then resentful from the constant pressure of his hand on the backs of their necks.

Well, if what I'm saying is to do more with less, then is there any way to say how much less? Is it possible to take this right to its absurd logical conclusion and say, "Don't cut at all?" Now we've come back to our first problem: Film is cut for practical reasons *and* film is cut because cutting—that sudden disruption of reality—can be an effective tool in itself. So, if the goal is as few cuts as possible, when you *have* to make a cut, what is it that makes it a good one?

The Rule of Six

*T*he first thing discussed in film-school editing classes is what I'm going to call three-dimensional continuity: In shot A, a man opens a door, walks halfway across the room, and then the film cuts to the next shot, B, picking him up at that same halfway point and continuing with him the rest of the way across the room, where he sits down at his desk, or something.

For many years, particularly in the early years of sound film, that was the rule. You struggled to preserve continuity of three-dimensional space, and it was seen as a failure of rigor or skill to violate it.[9] Jumping people around in space was just not done, except, perhaps, in extreme circumstances—fights or earthquakes—where there was a lot of violent action going on.

I actually place this three-dimensional continuity at the bottom of a list of six *criteria* for what makes a

---

[9] The problem with this thinking can be seen in any multi-camera situation-comedy on television. Because the cameras are filming simultaneously, the actors are necessarily always "correct" as far as their spatial continuity and relation to each other is concerned, but that absolutely does not prevent bad cuts from being made all the time.

good cut. At the top of the list is Emotion, the thing you come to last, if at all, at film school largely because it's the hardest thing to define and deal with. *How do you want the audience to feel?* If they are feeling what you want them to feel all the way through the film, you've done about as much as you can ever do. What they finally remember is not the editing, not the camerawork, not the performances, not even the story—it's how they felt.

An ideal cut (for me) is the one that satisfies all the following six criteria at once: 1) it is true to the emotion of the moment; 2) it advances the story; 3) it occurs at a moment that is rhythmically interesting and "right"; 4) it acknowledges what you might call "eye-trace"—the concern with the location and movement of the audience's focus of interest within the frame; 5) it respects "planarity"—the grammar of three dimensions transposed by photography to two (the questions of stage-line, etc.); 6) and it respects the three-dimensional continuity of the actual space (where people are in the room and in relation to one another).

Remember this, Fernando, if nothing else

1) Emotion	51%
2) Story	23%
3) Rhythm	10%
4) Eye-trace	7%
5) Two-dimensional plane of screen	5%
6) Three-dimensional space of action	4%

Emotion, at the top of the list, is the thing that you should try to preserve at all costs. If you find you have to sacrifice certain of those six things to make a cut, sacrifice your way up, item by item, from the bottom.

For instance, if you are considering a range of possible edits for a particular moment in the film, and you find that there is one cut that gives the right emotion *and* moves the story forward, *and* is rhythmically satisfying, *and* respects eye-trace and planarity, *but* it fails to preserve the continuity of three-dimensional space, then, by all means, that is the cut you should make. If none of the other edits has the right emotion, then sacrificing spatial continuity is well worth it.

The values I put after each item are slightly tongue-in-cheek, but not completely: Notice that the top two on the list (emotion and story) are worth far more than the bottom four (rhythm, eye-trace, planarity, spatial continuity), and when you come right down to it, under most circumstances, the top of the list—emotion—is worth more than all five of the things underneath it.

And, in fact, there is a practical side to this, which is that if the emotion is right and the story is advanced in a unique, interesting way, in the right rhythm, the audience will tend to be unaware of (or unconcerned about) editorial problems with lower-order items like eye-trace, stage-line, spatial continuity, etc. The general principle seems to be that satisfying the criteria of items higher on the list tends to obscure problems with items lower on the list, but not vice-versa: For instance, getting Number 4 (eye-trace) working properly will minimize a problem with Number 5 (stage-line), whereas if Number 5 (stage-line) is correct but

Number 4 (eye-trace) is not taken into consideration, the cut will be unsuccessful.

Now, in practice, you will find that those top three things on the list—emotion, story, rhythm—are extremely tightly connected. The forces that bind them together are like the bonds between the protons and neutrons in the nucleus of the atom. Those are, by far, the tightest bonds, and the forces connecting the lower three grow progressively weaker as you go down the list.

Most of the time you will be able to satisfy all six criteria: the three-dimensional space and the two-dimensional plane of the screen and the eye-trace, and the rhythm and story and emotion will all fall into place. And, of course, you should always aim for this, if possible—never accept less when more is available to you.

What I'm suggesting is a list of priorities. If you have to give up something, don't ever give up emotion before story. Don't give up story before rhythm, don't give up rhythm before eye-trace, don't give up eye-trace before planarity, and don't give up planarity before spatial continuity.

Misdirection

*U*nderlying these considerations is the central pre-occupation of a film editor, which should be to put himself/herself in place of the audience. What is the audience going to be thinking at any particular moment? Where are they going to be looking? What do you want them to think about? What do they need to think about? And, of course, what do you want them to feel? If you keep this in mind (and it's the preoccupation of every magician), then you are a kind of magician. Not in the supernatural sense, just an everyday, working magician.

Houdini's job was to create a sense of wonder, and to do that he didn't want you to look *here* (to the right) because that's where he was undoing his chains, so he found a way to make you look *there* (to the left). He was "misdirecting" you, as magicians say. He was doing something that would cause ninety-nine percent of you to look over here when he wanted you to. And an editor can do that and does do that—and *should* do that.

Sometimes, though, you can get caught up in the details and lose track of the overview. When that happens to me, it is usually because I have been looking at the image as the miniature it is in the editing room, rather than seeing it as the mural that it will become when projected in a theater. Something that will quickly restore the correct perspective is to imagine yourself very small, and the screen very large, and pretend that you are watching the finished film in a thousand-seat theater filled with people, and that the film is beyond the possibility of any further changes. If you still like what you see, it is probably okay. If not, you will now most likely have a better idea of how to correct the problem, whatever it is. One of the tricks I use to help me achieve this perspective is to cut out little paper dolls—a man and a woman—and put one on each side of the editing screen: The size of the dolls (a few inches high) is proportionately correct to make the screen seem as if it is thirty feet wide.

Seeing Around the Edge of the Frame

*T*he film editor is one of the few people working on the production of a film who does not know the exact conditions under which it was shot (or has the *ability* not to know) *and* who can at the same time have a tremendous influence on the film.

If you have been on and around the set most of the time, as the actors, the producer, director, cameraman, art director, etc., have been, you can get caught up in the sometimes bloody practicalities of gestation and delivery. And then when you see the dailies, you can't help, in your mind's eye, seeing around the edge of the frame—you can imagine everything that was there, physically and emotionally, just beyond what was actually photographed.

"We worked like hell to get that shot, it has to be in the film." You (the director, in this case) are convinced that what you got was what you wanted, but there's a possibility that you may to forcing yourself to see it that way because it cost so much—in money, time, angst—to get it.

By the same token, there are occasions when you shoot something that you dislike, when everyone is in a bad mood, and you say under protest: "All right, I'll do this, we'll get this one close-up, and then it's a wrap." Later on, when you look at that take, all you can remember was the hateful moment it was shot, and so you may be blind to the potentials it might have in a different context.

The editor, on the other hand, should try to see only what's on the screen, as the audience will. Only in this way can the images be freed from the context of their creation. By focusing on the screen, the editor will, hopefully, use the moments that should be used, even if they may have been shot under duress, and reject moments that should be rejected, even though they cost a terrible amount of money and pain.

I guess I'm urging the preservation of a certain kind of virginity. Don't *unnecessarily* allow yourself to be impregnated by the conditions of shooting. Try to keep up with what's going on but try to have as little specific knowledge of it as possible because, ultimately, the audience knows nothing about any of this—and you are the ombudsman for the audience.

The director, of course, is the person most familiar with all of the things that went on during the shoot, so he is the most burdened with this surplus, beyond-the-frame information. Between the end of shooting and before the first cut is finished, the very best thing that can happen to the director (and the film) is that he say goodbye to everyone and disappear for two weeks— up to the mountains or down to the sea or out to Mars or somewhere—and try to discharge this surplus.

Wherever he goes, he should try to think, as much as possible, about things that have absolutely nothing to do with the film. It is difficult, but it is necessary to create a barrier, a cellular wall between shooting and editing. Fred Zinnemann would go climbing in the Alps after the end of shooting, just to put himself in a potentially life-threatening situation where he had to be *there*, not day-dreaming about the film's problems.

Then, after a few weeks, he would come down from the Alps, back to earth; he would sit down in a dark room, alone, the arc light would ignite, and he would watch his film. He would still be, inherently, brimming with those images from beyond the edge of the frame (a director will never be fully able to forget them), but if he had gone straight from shooting to editing, the confusion would be worse and he would have gotten the two different thought processes of shooting and editing irrevocably mixed up.

Do everything you can to help the director erect this barrier for himself so that when he first sees the film, he can say, "All right, I'm going to pretend that I had nothing to do with this film. It needs some work. What needs to be done?"

And so you try as hard as you can to separate out what you wish from what is actually there, never abandoning your ultimate dreams for the film, but trying as hard as you can to see what is actually on the screen.

Dreaming in Pairs

*I*n many ways, the film editor performs the same role for the director as the text editor does for the writer of a book—to encourage certain courses of action, to counsel against others, to discuss whether to include specific material in the finished work or whether new material needs to be added. At the end of the day, though, it is the writer who then goes off and puts the words together.

But in film, the editor also has the responsibility for actually assembling the images (that is to say, the "words") in a certain order and in a certain rhythm. And here it becomes the *director's* role to offer advice and counsel much as he would to an actor interpreting a part. So it seems that the film editor/director relationship oscillates back and forth during the course of the project, the numerator becoming the denominator and vice versa.

In dream therapy there is a technique that pairs the patient—the *dreamer*, in this case—with someone who is there to *listen* to the dream. As soon as possible after waking, the dreamer gets together with his listener to review the dreams of the previous night.

Frequently there is nothing, or just a single disappointing image, but this is usually enough to begin the process. Once the image is described, the listener's job is to propose an imaginary sequence of events based on that fragment. An airplane, for instance, is all that is remembered. The listener immediately proposes that it must have been an airliner flying over Tahiti filled with golf balls for a tournament in Indonesia. No sooner has this description been offered than the dreamer finds himself protesting: "No, it was a biplane, flying over the battlefields of France, and Hannibal was shooting arrows at it from his legion of elephants." In other words, the dream itself, hidden in the memory, rises to its own defense when it hears itself being challenged by an alternate version, and so reveals itself. This revelation about bi-planes and elephants can in turn prompt the listener to elaborate another improvisation, which will coax out another aspect of the hidden dream, and so on, until as much of the dream is revealed as possible.

The relationship between director and editor is somewhat similar in that the director is generally the dreamer and the editor is the listener. But even for the most well-prepared of directors, there are limits to the imagination and memory, particularly at the level of fine detail, and so it is the editor's job to propose alternate scenarios as bait to encourage the sleeping dream to rise to its defense and thus reveal itself more fully. And these scenarios unfold themselves at the largest level (should such-and-such a scene be removed from the film for the good of the whole?) and at the most detailed (should this shot end on this frame or 1/24th of a second later on the *next* frame?). But sometimes it is the editor who is the dreamer and the director who is the listener, and it is he who now offers the bait to tempt the collective dream to reveal more of itself.

As any fisherman can tell you, it is the quality of the bait that determines the kind of fish you catch.

Team Work: Multiple Editors

*N*ot only does the editor collaborate with the director, there are frequent times when two or more editors are working simultaneously, sometimes with equal authority. This seems odd to many people, who do not see the same thing happening with directors of photography or production designers. But for some reason, which has to do with the collaborative mentality of editors and with the fact that the time pressure of post-production is not quite so unforgiving in its consequences as it is during production, multiple editors are often employed. I have worked, and enjoyed, collaborating with other editors on many films: *The Conversation, Apocalypse Now, The Unbearable Lightness of Being,* and *Godfather, Part III.*

The main advantage to collaborative editing is speed; the main risk is lack of coherence. But if there are upward of 350,000 feet of workprint (sixty-five hours), you are probably going to need to take that risk and have two editors, or at least an associate editor working under supervision. But problems can sometimes arise if there is just one editor on a film and he develops a locked viewpoint about the material. This is particularly troublesome if the director and the editor have not worked together before and have no time to develop a common language. In this case, it might not be a bad idea to consider having multiple editors.

The Godfather was the first film on which Francis worked with two editors. Originally there had been just a single editor, but the problem of locked viewpoint became acute and he was let go after several months. The decision was made to reconstitute what had been done up to that point and start again, but because they had effectively lost those months, and it looked as though the film was going to be almost three hours long with an inflexible deadline, it made sense to hire two editors. The film was still shooting and there was just a lot of work to do: Each editor had a ninety-minute film to complete in twenty-four weeks. But unlike the later *Godfather, Part II* or *Apocalypse*, the work was split strictly in half. Bill Reynolds cut the first part and Peter Zinner cut the last part. There's a specific point where Bill's section ends and Peter's begins.

On *Godfather, Part II*, although the responsibility for editing was divided up in a checkerboard pattern, scenes were initially cut and recut by the same person.[10] But when Francis began to play with the structure of the film, people found themselves recutting what others had originally edited.

---

[10] The editors of *Godfather, Part II,* were Peter Zinner, Barry Malkin, and Richard Marks.

The interest on a $25 million film is around $250,000 a month. If having two editors can help you release that film a month earlier, they will have repaid a good portion, if not all, of their salaries for the whole film. It is simply a matter of how much you want to achieve in the time you have available. If you end up with a cut-per-day rate of 1.47, as we did on *Apocalypse*, that means that many different avenues have been explored to get to the final product. If that's what you want to do, you probably need more than one editor.

The Decisive Moment

While Phil Kaufman was shooting *The Unbear-able Lightness of Being* in France, I was edit-ing it in Berkeley, California—6,000 miles away. The dailies would be shipped approximately every two weeks, and I would then sit and watch ten hours or so of film, taking notes, making sure it was in sync, getting ready to code it, etc.

But in addition to the usual procedures, I also would select at least one representative frame from every setup (camera position) and take a still photo-graph of it off the workprint. We then had these pho-tos developed and printed at the local "one hour" place, like family snapshots, and they were put onto panels arranged according to scene. Whenever a setup had complex staging or a moving camera, it was nec-essary to take more than one photo (I think the most that I ever took for *Unbearable* was seven, which was for a very complicated party scene)—usually it was three, and most of the time it was just one.

We had to use a special reproducing negative to make these pictures, since an ordinary snapshot nega-tive produces too much contrast. The speed of the film is low—about ASA 2 or something—so the time exposure has to be quite long, but it worked out well: The photos were actually pretty close approximations of the real color balance and contrast ratio of the film.

The photographs are a great help in later discussions with the director about what was shot and how it was shot—they resolve those kinds of discussions very quickly.

They also provide a record of some details beyond the ability of even the best continuity person: The particulars of an actor's hairline, or a little peculiarity of costume, the way the collar flips up or down, or how rosy somebody's complexion was, or whether their hat left a mark on their forehead when they took it off—those kinds of things.

They are also a great resource for the publicity department or anyone else coming onto the film at a later date. You can instantly see and cross-reference characters in all kinds of different emotional states, as well as the photography, the costumes, and the scenery.

Also, just because of the way they were displayed, the pictures tended to collide against each other in interesting ways. On *Unbearable*, we had perhaps sixteen panels of photos, 130 photos to a panel, and each panel was laid out like a page of a book: You "read" the photos from left to right and then down a row, left to right again, etc., just like reading text, and when you got to the bottom of one panel, you went up to the top of the next and read

Two frames of Teresa (played by Juliette Binoche) from *The Unbearable Lightness of Being*. The three-digit numbers in the lower left-hand corner of each picture (620, 296) refer to the setup number of the shot from which the frame was taken, and the number (2.2) in the adjacent rectangle of #620 identifies that frame as occupying a certain place in the sequence—frame two in a series of two.

Two frames of Sabina (played by Lena Olin) from *The
Unbearable Lightness of Being.* The numbering system
here is the same as for Teresa's photos on the previous
pages. Both these frames come from the impromptu photo
session between Sabina and Teresa.

Two frames of Teresa from *The Unbearable Lightness of Being*. In the case of #542, one frame was sufficient to give a complete idea of the setup. Number 635, however, required three photos—of which this is number two—because of the complex nature of the shot. This comes from the same scene as #634 of Sabina and the two shots were cut together in the finished film.

across the first line, etc. So the juncture *between* those panels was an interesting thing to look at, because it juxtaposed frames that were never meant to go together and yet there they were, right next to each other. And sometimes you got sparks out of that, it would cause you to think about things, editorial leaps, that otherwise you might never have thought of without this system.

But the most interesting asset of the photos for me was that they provided the hieroglyphs for a language of emotions.

What word expresses the concept of ironic anger tinged with melancholy? There isn't a word for it, in English anyway, but you can see that specific emotion represented in this photograph.

Or the photo may represent a kind of nervous anticipation: The character is scared and lustful at the same time, and yet she is confused because that lust is for another woman. And that woman is sleeping with her husband. So what does that mean?

Whatever it means, it is there in her expression, in the angle of her head and her hair and her neck and the tension in the muscles and the set of her mouth and what is in her eyes. And if you can simply point to an expression on an actor's face, you have a way around some of the difficulties of language in dealing with the subtleties of nameless emotions. You, as the director, can say, "That's what I want. The sequence we are working on should have more of that, you know. I want it to embody the nameless but familiar emotion I see in that photograph."

The editor's job now is to choose the right images and make those images follow one another at the right rate to express something like what is captured in that photograph.

In choosing a representative frame, what you're looking for is an image that distills the essence of the thousands of frames that make up the shot in question, what Cartier-Bresson—referring to still photography—called the "decisive moment." So I think, more often than not, the image that I chose wound up in the film. And also, more often than not, quite close to the cut point.

When you look at dailies, there's a pitfall similar to the one that you may fall into during casting sessions. For the actor who is walking through the door, this casting session is the one and only time that he is going to present him or herself to you. This is a tremendously important moment for him, but for you, this may be the sixtieth person you've seen that day. Inevitably there is a kind of mental glaze that may form after a while that stops you thinking as sharply as you should.

Well, dailies are like that, too. Each shot is auditioning for your approval. Take five: "How about me? I can do this." Then take seven comes in the door: "How about this?" Take nine: "Or this?"

And to keep your awareness, to really be alive to the possibilities in each shot, you have to keep jabbing yourself. You try to remain fresh and see the wonderful things and make records of those as well as the things that may not be so wonderful. Which is what you have to do when you are casting a film.

But if you have to choose a representative set of stills from every setup, you will automatically start thinking differently—you have to be analytical right from the beginning, which is what you should be when you are looking at dailies. But, everyone being human and dailies sometimes going on as long as they do, we sometimes tend to just sit there and let the dailies roll over us. What this photo system does is just tip you up out of your chair a bit. It is an encouragement to do what you should be doing anyway. And it is the beginning of the editorial process. You are already beginning to edit at the point that you say, "I like this frame rather than that frame."

Methods and Machines: Marble and Clay

*T*he tools you choose to edit with can have a determining effect on the final product. But when I started editing in 1965, there was really just one option, at least in Hollywood: the Moviola, a "standup" editing machine—virtually unchanged since the 1930s—that looks something like a sewing machine (and sounds like one). In the early days of Zoetrope Studios, which was founded on a European model, we used imported Steenbecks or KEMs, "horizontal" editing machines from Germany that were quieter and handled the film more gently, had two large screens and two sound tracks, and were better able to handle large amounts of film. Now, of course, the landscape has been permanently altered by the computer—electronic digital editing machines, such as Avid and Lightworks, that harness together a video display terminal and a computer with a large-scale memory bank where the film's images and sounds can be stored digitally.[11]

---

[11] For a more complete survey of the current non-linear systems, see the Afterword: Non-Linear Digital Editing—The Unbearable Lightness.

I feel equally comfortable working on a Moviola, a KEM Universal, or an Avid. It depends on the film, the film's budget and schedule, and on my hunch about the style of the director and how long the average take is going to be. *The Conversation* was edited on a KEM, *Julia* on a Moviola, *Apocalypse Now* on a KEM, whereas I used both on *Unbearable*—it started out on a Moviola and changed to a KEM. With the KEM, I arrange things opposite of the way they are normally done, so that the screen directly in front of me is my search screen and the soundtrack in front of me is in sync with that. The screen on the left side and the sound on the right side are in sync with each other and hold the assembled film. If I were working on a bench, that would be what's going through the synchronizer.

In fact, speaking of benches, I should add that I work standing up: My KEM is raised about fifteen inches off the floor to put it at the right height for me. One of the things I always liked about the Moviola is that you stand up to work, holding the Moviola in a kind of embrace—dancing with it, in a way—so it was frustrating for me to have to sit down at the KEM. I edited both *The Conversation* and *Apocalypse* that way, sitting down, but a voice in the back of my head kept telling me something wasn't quite right. And so when I came to edit *Unbearable,* I had the KEM raised up on two plywood boxes.

Editing is a kind of surgery—and have you ever seen a surgeon sitting to perform an operation? Editing is also like cooking—and no one sits down at the stove to cook. But most of all, editing is a kind of dance—the finished film is a kind of crystallized dance—and when have you ever seen a dancer sitting down to dance?

Other than the "standing/sitting" question, the differences between the Moviola system and the KEM system boil down to sculptural ones: The Moviola system "emulsifies" the film into little bits (individual shots) and then the editor reassembles it out of those bits, like making something out of clay. You take a little bit of clay and you stick it here and you take another little bit of clay and you stick it *there*. At the beginning of the process there is nothing in front of you, then there is something in front of you, and then there is finally the finished thing all built up out of little clay bricks, little pellets of information.

With the KEM system, I don't ever break the film down into individual shots—I leave it in ten-minute rolls in the order in which it came from the lab. In sculptural terms, this is like a block of marble—the sculpture is already there, hidden within the stone, and you reveal it by taking away, rather than building it up piece by piece from nothing, as you do with clay. It is really the difference between "random-access" editing and its opposite, whatever that is called—"linear-access," let's say.

Computerized digital editing and, strangely enough, good old-fashioned Moviola editing with an assistant, are both random-access, non-linear systems: You ask for something specific and that thing—that thing alone—is delivered to you as quickly as possible. You are only shown what you ask for. The Avid is faster at it than the Moviola, but the process is the same.

That's a drawback for me because your choices can then only be as good as your requests, and sometimes that is not enough. There is a higher level that comes through *recognition*: You may not be able to articulate what you want, but you can recognize it when you see it.

What do I mean by that? Well, if you learn to speak a foreign language, you will find that there is a gap between how well you can speak it and how well you can understand it when it is spoken to you. A human being's ability to understand a foreign language is always greater than his ability to speak it.

And when you make a film, you are trying to learn a foreign language—it just happens to be a unique language that is only spoken by this one film. If you have to articulate everything, as you do with a random-access system like video/computer or Moviola/ assistant, you are limited by what and how much you can articulate and how good your original notes were. Whereas the advantage of the KEM's linear system is that I do not always have to be speaking to it—there are times when *it* speaks to *me*. The system is constantly presenting things for consideration, and a sort of dialogue takes place. I might say, "I want to see that close-up of Teresa, number 317, in roll 45." But I'll put that roll on the machine, and as I spool down to number 317 (which may be hundreds of feet from the start), the machine shows me everything at high speed down to that point, saying in effect: "How about this instead? Or this?" And I find, more often than not, long before I get down to shot 317, that I've had three other ideas triggered by the material that I have seen flashing by me.

"Oh, this other shot is much better than the one I thought I wanted." As soon as I saw it, I recognized it as a possibility, whereas I couldn't articulate it as a choice.

When you look at dailies the first time, you have a relatively fixed idea—based on the script—of what you are looking for. Later on, though, you review some of your original notes, and they will say, for instance: "212-4: NG." What does that mean? It meant that *at the time* you thought take four of Slate 212 was No Good, and you didn't bother to make a note of why you thought so. Well, many times in the re-editing, what you thought was originally unusable may come to be your salvation.

If it was a question of only one shot, or two dozen shots, you could probably deal with the problem of second-guessing those original notes, but, in fact, an ordinary film will have 700, 1,000, 2,000 setups with more than two printed takes per setup on average, and so there may easily be two to four thousand shots that you have to have an opinion about. That's a lot of second-guessing, so you tend to fall back on your first impressions in the original notes. Which are valuable, but limited, if that is all you have.

Whereas with the KEM system, because the film is all stored in these big rolls in an *almost* arbitrary way, you are learning something new about the material as you search for what you think you want. You are actually doing creative work, and you may find what you *really* want rather than what you *thought* you wanted. This system is useful enough in the original assembly of the scene, in helping you to familiarize yourself with the material, but it becomes particularly valuable in the recutting, where your original notes—heavily influenced by the script—become less and less useful as the film finds its own voice.

There are limits, of course: A system that is too linear (which means that you have to spend too much time searching before you find what you want) would be burdensome. You would quickly become overwhelmed and/or bored with it. So there is a golden mean somewhere. If the system is completely random-access, that is a defect, in my opinion. But if it is too linear, that's a defect as well. What I've found, personally, is that given the attitude I have toward the material, given the speed that I work, and given the mechanical speed of the KEM itself, keeping the dailies in ten-minute reels in shooting order adds just about the right amount of chaos that I need in order to work the way I want to.

The digital systems, Avid and Lightworks, are promising because they offer the potential to merge the best of the Moviola's non-linear approach with the best of the KEM's ability to handle and review large amounts of material quickly. At this point, there is still some procedural awkwardness with the digital systems, but I expect those to be smoothed out over time.

In any case, there are certain things that remain the same for me no matter what system I am using. I would always review the material twice: once at the beginning, the day after the material was shot, noting down my first impressions and including any notes the director cares to give me. And then when I was ready to cut a particular scene, I would collect all the relevant material and review it again, making notes in more detail than the first time.

When you look at rushes the second time, you have evolved and the film has evolved. You will see different things than you saw the first time, because you may have assembled scenes that hadn't been shot the first time you saw the material, and strengths or problems may be emerging with characters and events as they unfold.

In an ideal world, what I would like to do is assemble a first cut and then stop and just look at all the dailies again, fresh. Whether I would ever actually be able to do that is another question: The present schedule of films, at any rate, prohibits such a thing. This is where the hidden virtues of the linear (KEM) system come in—because of the way the material is stored, in ten-minute rolls of film, it is constantly being reviewed. If this were gardening, I would be talking about the virtues of turning over the soil and aerating it.

In the actual editing of a scene, I will keep on working until I can no longer "see myself" in the material. When I review my first assembly of a scene, more often than not I can still vividly (too vividly!) recall making the decisions that led to each of the cuts. But as the scene is reworked and refined, it reaches a point, hopefully, where the shots themselves seem to create each other: This shot "makes" the next shot, which "makes" the next shot, etc. In this way, the Walter Murch who decided things initially gradually recedes until, finally, there comes a point where he has become invisible and the characters take over, the shots, the emotion, the story seem to take over. Sometimes—the best times—this process reaches the point where I can look at the scene and say, "I didn't have anything to do with that—it just created itself."

As far as the color balance of the final prints goes, I've had a few good experiences, but many have been frustrating for one reason or another. The worst thing is that the labs show the film at twenty-four frames per second (and sometimes even at thirty-two fps) without the ability to stop or go backward. You are sitting there and saying: "That shot should be redder." "Which one?" "The close-up of the foot." But already eight shots have gone by. Most often, the impression you get is that they are doing this as a courtesy just to keep you quiet.

One way that works for me, where you can really see what's going on and get specific with your notes about color, is to take the workprint and the first answer print and put them in sync over a light box of the correct color temperature. There is something about a low level of light coming through a piece of film that enables you to see tonalities that are almost invisible if you're looking at a bright screen of projected light. There may be a residual greenness, you know, but you look at the film in a viewing theater and you'll say, "I don't know. Is that shot a little green? Or is it too blue?" And, of course, before you have decided, you are looking at something else. If you work with the light-box system, the green will just leap out, especially if you've got your original workprint there for comparison. And you can stop, go forward, go backward, etc.

If you are fortunate enough to be working with a good color timer at a good laboratory, of course, it is like any sort of successful collaboration.

Test Screenings:
Referred Pain

*T*oward the end of the editing process on *Julia*, Fred Zinnemann observed that he felt the director and the editor, alone with the film for months and months, could only go ninety percent of the way toward the finished film—that what was needed for the last ten percent was "the participation of the audience," whom he saw as his final collaborators. Not in the sense that he would respond to them blindly, but that he felt their presence was helpful as a corrective, to keep certain obsessions from becoming corrosive and to point out blind spots that may have developed through over-familiarity with the material.

This has certainly been my experience: All of the films I have worked on have been tested before large audiences except for *The Conversation* and *Unbearable Lightness.* We had screenings of them, of course, but we never had wide-open, public screenings. Francis Coppola in particular has always been an enthusiastic supporter of screening his films almost at any stage, almost no matter how unfinished they were.

Rough screenings would be for small groups of about ten people whom he knew, mixed with two or three people who were strangers. The strangers would have no previous idea of what this film was about, and he would question them afterward, on a one-to-one basis, to compare their opinions to the reaction of the people who did know about the film.

Fred Zinnemann, by contrast, would show *Julia* to a preview audience only when it was technically completely finished, with a cut negative and optical sound track. He was perfectly prepared to change it after that, but he doesn't believe that general audiences can completely discount visible splices, color mismatches, and incomplete sound tracks, and I agree with him.

Even with technically finished films, public previews are tricky things. You can learn a tremendous amount from them, but you have to be cautious about direct interpretations of what people have to say to you, particularly on those cards they fill out after the screening. I'm extremely suspicious of those. The most helpful thing of all is simply learning how *you* feel when the film is being shown to 600 people who have never seen it before. Emotionally, it seems like some big hand has come and grabbed you by the hair, picked you up, and put you down ninety degrees to one side. And you think, "Oh God, look at *that.*" It's as if up to this moment you have been constructing a building but always standing in front of it to evaluate it. Now all of a sudden you are looking at the side of the building and seeing things you seem to have never seen before.

You shouldn't blindly follow what you learn from these test screenings any more than you should anything else. What can you learn from the differences *between* the previous screenings and this one? Given these two headings, where is the North Pole? Test screenings are just a way to find out where you are.

There was one procedure on *Julia* that, unfortunately, I have never seen repeated. We had a person sitting at a table in the lobby of the preview theater with a sign in front of him that said, "If you want to talk to us on the telephone after a few days, leave your number here." And then those conversations were transcribed and added into the survey. If you are going to do previews and listen to what people have to say, that's the way to do it—after they have had a day or two to let the film sink in. Don't look at what people write in the heat of the moment—you get a reaction, but it is a skewed reaction. There's a lot of what is medically called "referred pain" in that process.

When you go to a doctor and tell him that you have a pain in your elbow, it is the quack who takes out his scalpel and starts to operate on the elbow. Then you wind up with not only the original pain but probably a pain in your wrist and your shoulder as well. Whereas an experienced doctor studies you, takes an x-ray, and determines that the cause of the pain is probably a pinched nerve up in your shoulder—you just happen to feel it in your elbow. The pain in the shoulder has been "referred" to the elbow. Audience reactions are like that. When you ask the direct question, "What was your least favorite scene?" and eighty percent of the people are in agreement about one scene they do not like, the impulse is to "fix" the scene or cut it out. But the chances are that that scene is fine. Instead, the problem may be that the audience simply didn't understand something that they needed to know for the scene to work.

So, instead of fixing the scene itself, you might clarify some exposition that happens five minutes earlier. Don't necessarily operate on the elbow: instead, discover if nerves are being pinched somewhere else. But the audience will never tell you that directly. They will simply tell you where the pain is, not the source of the pain.

Editing decisions become particularly acute in the last days before the film is released, since changes made now will be permanent. If you, as the editor, have a particularly strong feeling about something at this stage, you should try to make your point as forcefully and convincingly as you can—perhaps you stay late and do a test version of your idea, sketch something out—but you also need to have discretion, a sense of who you are dealing with, and present your ideas to the director or producer in the right context. And how you go about this has to do with your whole working history, how you were hired, how much you respect the director, how much the director respects you.

I remember one moment particularly, after the previews of *Julia*, when Fred Zinnemann and I were debating what final changes to make in the structure of the beginning, which seemed to have been difficult for the audience to follow. The opening reel of the film had a nested sequence of flashbacks—a

memory of a memory of a memory of a memory—
and it was perhaps one too many. I suggested eliminating of one scene that occupied a unique time-frame
in the film's structure (one that was never reprised),
and we decided to remove this, since it meant that
the scenes that were left would consequently sort
themselves into a more graspable sequence. As I was
undoing the splices (and they made a little screech as
they came apart, almost as if they were crying out in
pain), Zinnemann looked thoughtfully at what was
happening and observed in an almost offhand way,
"You know, when I first read this scene in the script,
I knew that I could do this film."

I hesitated briefly, looked at him, and then continued undoing the splices. But my heart was in my
throat because at that stage in the process you do not
know; you can only have *faith* that what you are doing
is the right thing. Were we mistakenly cutting out the
heart of the film, or were we snipping off the umbilical cord?

In retrospect, I believe it *was* the umbilical cord
and that we were right to remove it: The scene did
have an essential function at one point, which was to
connect Fred Zinnemann to the project, but once that
connection had been made and Zinnemann's sensi-
bility had flowed through that scene into all the other
scenes in the film, it could finally be removed without any harm.

But things like that do give you pause.

Don't Worry, It's Only a Movie

Earlier I asked the question, "Why do cuts work?" We *know* that they do. And yet it is still surprising when you think about it because of the violence of what is actually taking place: At the instant of the cut, there is a total and instantaneous discontinuity of the field of vision.

I recall once coming back to the editing room after a few weeks in the mixing theater (where all movements are smooth and incremental) and being appalled at the brutality of the process of cutting. The "patient" is pinned to the slab and: Whack! Either/Or! This not That! In or Out! We chop up the poor film in a miniature guillotine and then stick the dismembered pieces together like Dr. Frankenstein's monster. The difference (the miraculous difference) is that out of this apparent butchery our creation can sometimes gain not only a life but a soul as well. It is all the more amazing because the instantaneous displacement achieved by the cut is not anything that we experience in ordinary life.

We are accustomed to such things, of course, in music (Beethoven was the innovator and master of this) as well as in our own thoughts—the way one realization will suddenly overwhelm everything else, to be, in turn, replaced by yet another. But in the dramatic arts—theater, ballet, opera—there didn't seem to be any way to achieve total instantaneous displacement: stage machinery can only move so fast, after all. *So why do cuts work?* Do they have some hidden foundation in our own experience, or are they an invention that suits the convenience of filmmakers and people have just, somehow, become used to them?

Well, although "day-to-day" reality appears to be continuous, there *is* that other world in which we spend perhaps a third of our lives: the "night-to-night" reality of dreams. And the images in dreams are much more fragmented, intersecting in much stranger and more abrupt ways than the images of waking reality—ways that approximate, at least, the interaction produced by cutting.

Perhaps the explanation is as simple as that: We accept the cut because it resembles the way images are juxtaposed in our dreams. In fact, the abruptness of the cut may be one of the key determinants in actually *producing* the similarity between films and dreams. In the darkness of the theater, we say to ourselves, in effect, "This looks like reality, but it cannot be reality because it is so visually discontinuous; therefore, it must be a dream."

(Along those lines, it is revealing that the words a parent uses to comfort a child frightened by a nightmare—"Don't worry, darling, it's only a dream"—are almost the same words used to comfort a child frightened by a film—"Don't worry, darling, it's only a movie." Frightening dreams and films have a similar power to overwhelm the defenses that are otherwise effective against equally frightening books, paintings, music. For instance, it is hard to imagine this phrase: "Don't worry, darling, it's only a painting.")

The problem with all this is that the comparison of films and dreams is interesting, probably true, but relatively barren of practical fruits: We still know so little about the nature of dreams that the observation comes to a stop once it has been made.

Something to consider, though, is the possibility that there may be a part of our waking reality where we actually do experience something like cuts, and where daylight images are somehow brought in closer, more discontinuous, juxtaposition than might otherwise seem to be the case.

I began to get a glimmer of this on my first picture-editing job—*The Conversation* (1974)—when I kept finding that Gene Hackman (Harry Caul in the film) would blink very close to the point where I had decided to cut. It was interesting, but I didn't know what to make of it.

Then, one morning after I had been working all night, I went out to get some breakfast and happened to walk past the window of a Christian Science Reading Room, where the front page of the *Monitor* featured an interview with John Huston. I stopped to read it, and one thing struck me forcefully because it related exactly to this question of the blink:

"To me, the perfect film is as though it were unwinding behind your eyes, and your eyes were projecting it themselves, so that you were seeing what you wished to see. Film is like thought. It's the closest to thought process of any art.

"Look at that lamp across the room. Now look back at me. Look back at that lamp. Now look back at me again. Do you see what you did? You *blinked.* Those are *cuts.* After the first look, you know that there's no reason to pan continuously from me to the lamp because you know what's in between. Your mind cut the scene. First you behold the lamp. *Cut.* Then you behold me."[12]

What Huston asks us to consider is a physiological mechanism—the blink—that interrupts the apparent visual continuity of our perceptions: My head may move smoothly from one side of the room to the other, but, in fact, I am cutting the flow of visual images into significant bits, the better to juxtapose and compare those bits—"lamp" and "face" in Huston's example—without irrelevant information getting in the way.

Of course there are limits to the kind of juxtapositions I can make this way—I can't jump forward or backward in time and space (that is the prerogative of dreams and films).[13] But even so, the visual displacements available to me just by turning my head (from the Grand Canyon in front of me to the forest behind me, or even from one side of this room to the other) are sometimes quite great.

---

[12] *Christian Science Monitor,* August 11, 1973. John Huston interviewed by Louise Sweeney.

[13] But see footnote #16.

After I read that article, I started observing people, watching when they blinked, and I began to discover something much different than what they tell you in high-school biology, which is that the blink is simply a means to moisten the surface of the eye. If that's all it is, then for each environment and each individual there would be a purely mechanical, predictable interval between blinks depending on the humidity, temperature, wind speed, etc. You would only blink when your eye began to get too dry, and that would be a constant number of seconds for each environment. This is clearly not the case: People will sometimes keep their eyes open for minutes at a time—at other times they will blink repeatedly—with many variations in between. The question then is, "What is causing them to blink?"

On the one hand, I'm sure you've all been confronted by someone who was so angry that he didn't blink at all: This is a person, I believe, in the grip of a single thought that he holds (and that holds him), inhibiting the urge and need to blink.[14] And then there is the opposite kind of anger that causes someone to blink every second or so: This time, the person is being assailed simultaneously by many conflicting emotions and thoughts, and is desperately (but unconsciously) using those blinks to try to separate these thoughts, sort things out, and regain some kind of control.

---

[14] There is that telling phrase from classic cowboy (and now diplomatic) stand-offs: "he blinked." The loser in this mental game of chicken could not hold fast to his single position and instead allowed some other thought to intrude at the critical moment. The blink signals the moment he relinquished his primary thought.

So it seems to me that our rate of blinking is somehow geared more to our emotional state and to the nature and frequency of our thoughts than to the atmospheric environment we happen to find ourselves in. Even if there is no head movement (as there was in Huston's example), the blink is either *something that helps an internal separation of thought to take place,* or it is *an involuntary reflex accompanying the mental separation that is taking place anyway.*[15]

And not only is the *rate* of blinking significant, but so is the actual *instant* of the blink itself. Start a conversation with somebody and watch when they blink. I believe you will find that your listener will blink at the precise moment he or she "gets" the idea of what you are saying, not an instant earlier or later. Why would this be? Well, speech is full of unobserved grace notes and elaborations—the conversational equivalents of "Dear Sir" and "Yours Sincerely"—and the essence of what we have to say is often sandwiched between an introduction and a conclusion. The blink will take place either when the listener realizes our "introduction" is finished and that now we are going to say something significant, or it will happen when he feels we are "winding down" and not going to say anything more significant for the moment.

And that blink will occur where a cut could have happened, had the conversation been filmed. Not a frame earlier or later.

So we entertain an idea, or a linked sequence of ideas, and we blink to separate and punctuate that idea from what follows. Similarly—in film—a shot

---

[15] Dr. John Stern of Washington University in St. Louis has recently (1987) published experimental work in the psycho-physiology of the blink that seems to confirm this.

presents us with an idea, or a sequence of ideas, and the cut is a "blink" that separates and punctuates those ideas.[16] At the moment you decide to cut, what you are saying is, in effect, "I am going to bring this idea to an end and start something new." It is important to emphasize that the cut by *itself* does not create the "blink moment"—the tail does not wag the dog. If the cut is well-placed, however, the more extreme the visual discontinuity—from dark interior to bright exterior, for instance—the more thorough the effect of punctuation will be.

At any rate, I believe "filmic" juxtapositions are taking place in the real world not only when we dream but also when we are awake. And, in fact, I would go so far as to say that these juxtapositions are not accidental mental artifacts but part of the method we use to make sense of the world: We must render visual reality discontinuous, otherwise perceived reality would resemble an almost incomprehensible string of letters without word separation or punctuation. When we sit in the dark theater, then we find edited film a (surprisingly) familiar experience. "More like thought than anything else," in Huston's words.[17]

---

[16] This can occur regardless of how big or small the "idea" happens to be. For instance, the idea could be as simple as "she moves quickly to the left."

[17] William Stokoe makes an intriguing comparison between the techniques of film editing and American Sign Language: "In signed language, narrative is no longer linear. Instead, the essence is to cut from a normal view to a close-up to a distant shot to a close-up again, even including flashback and flash-forward scenes, exactly as a movie editor works. Not only is signing arranged more like edited film than like written narration, but also each signer is placed very much as a camera: the field of vision and angle of view are directed but variable." William Stokoe, *Language in Four Dimensions*, New York Academy of Sciences (1979).

Dragnet

*I*f it is true that our rates and rhythms of blinking refer directly to the rhythm and sequence of our inner emotions and thoughts, then those rates and rhythms are insights into our inner selves and, therefore, as characteristic of each of us as our signatures. So if an actor is successful at projecting himself into the emotions and thoughts of a character, his blinks will *naturally and spontaneously* occur at the point that the character's blinks would have occurred in real life.[18]

I believe this is what I was finding with Hackman's performance in *The Conversation*—he had assumed the character of Harry Caul, was thinking a series of Harry's thoughts the way Harry would think them, and, therefore, was blinking in rhythm with those thoughts. And since I was absorbing the rhythms he

---

[18] One of the things about unsuccessful acting is that the actor's blinks seem to come at the "wrong" times. Although you may not notice this consciously, the rhythm of the actor's blinks don't match the rhythm of thoughts you would expect from the character he is playing. In fact, a bad actor is probably not thinking anything like what the character would be thinking. Instead: "I wonder what the director thinks of me, I wonder if I look okay," or "What's my next line?"

was giving me and trying to think similar thoughts myself, my cut points were naturally aligning themselves with his "blink points." In a sense, I had rerouted my neural circuitry so that the semi-involuntary command to blink caused me instead to hit the stop button on the editing machine.

To that same end, one of the disciplines I follow is to choose the "out point" of a shot by marking it in real time. If I can't do this—if I can't hit that same frame repeatedly at twenty-four frames per second— I know there is something wrong in my approach to the shot, and I adjust my thinking until I find a frame I *can* hit. I never permit myself to select the "out point" by inching back and forth, comparing one frame with another to get the best match. That method—for me, at any rate—is guaranteed to produce a rhythmic "tone deafness" in the film.

Anyway, another one of your tasks as an editor is this "sensitizing" of yourself to the rhythms that the (good) actor gives you, and then finding ways to extend these rhythms into territory not covered by the actor himself, so that the pacing of the film as a whole is an elaboration of those patterns of thinking and feeling. And one of the many ways you assume those rhythms is by noticing—consciously or unconsciously—where the actor blinks.

There is a way of editing that ignores all of these questions, what I would call the "Dragnet" system, from the 1950s TV series of the same name.

The policy of the show seemed to be to keep every word of dialogue on screen. When someone had finished speaking, there was a brief pause and then a cut to the person, who was now about to talk, and when he in turn finished speaking there was a cut back to the first person who nodded his head or said something, and then when *that* person was finished, they cut back again, etc. It extended to single words. "Have you been downtown yet?" *Cut.* "No." *Cut.* "When are you going downtown?" *Cut.* "Tomorrow." *Cut.* "Have you seen your son?" *Cut.* "No, he didn't come home last night." *Cut.* "What time does he usually come home?" *Cut.* "Two o'clock." At the time, when it first came out, this technique created a sensation for its apparently hard-boiled, police-blotter realism.

The "Dragnet" system is a simple way to edit, but it is a shallow simplicity that doesn't reflect the grammar of complex exchanges that go on all the time in even the most ordinary conversations. If you're observing a dialogue between two people, you will not focus your attention solely on the person who is speaking. Instead, while *that person is still talking,* you will turn to look at the listener to find out what he thinks of what is being said. The question is, "When exactly do you turn?"

There are places in a conversation where it seems we almost physically *cannot* blink or turn our heads (since we are still receiving important information), and there are other places where we *must* blink or turn away in order to make better sense of what we have received. And I would suggest that there are similar points in every scene where the cut *cannot* or *must* occur, and for the same reasons. Every shot has potential "cut points" the way a tree has branches, and once you have identified them, you will choose different points depending on what the audience has been thinking up to that moment and what you want them to think next.

For instance, by cutting away from a certain character *before* he finishes speaking, I might encourage the audience to think only about the face value of what he said. On the other hand, if I linger on the character *after* he finishes speaking, I allow the audience to see, from the expression in his eyes, that he is probably not telling the truth, and they will think differently about him and what he said. But since it takes a *certain amount of time* to make that observation, I cannot cut away from the character too early: Either I cut away while he is speaking (branch number one) or I hold until the audience realizes he is lying (branch number two), but *I cannot cut in between those two branches*—to do so would either seem too long or not long enough. The branch points are fixed organically by the rhythm of the shot itself and by what the audience has been thinking up to that moment in the film,[19] but I am free to select one or the other of them (or yet another one further on) depending on what realization I want the audience to make.

In this way, you should be able to cut from the speaker to the listener and vice versa in psychologically interesting, complex, and "correct" patterns that reflect the kinds of shifts of attention and realization that go on in real life: In this way, you establish a

---

[19] One way to shift the actual branch points themselves is to place the shot in a different context, where the audience will be thinking (and noticing) different things.

rhythm that counterpoints and underscores the ideas being expressed or considered. And one of the tools to identify exactly where these cut points, these "branches," may be is to compare them to our patterns of blinking, which have been underscoring the rhythm of our thoughts for tens of thousands, perhaps millions, of years of human history. Where you feel comfortable blinking—if you are really listening to what is being said—is where the cut will feel right.

So there are really three problems wrapped up together:

1) identifying a series of potential cut points (and comparisons with the blink can help you do this),

2) determining what effect each cut point will have on the audience, and

3) choosing which of those effects is the correct one for the film.

I believe the sequence of thoughts—that is to say, the rhythm and rate of cutting—should be appropriate to whatever the audience is watching at the moment. The average "real-world" rate of blinking is somewhere between the extremes of four and forty blinks per minute. If you are in an actual fight, you will be blinking dozens of times a minute because you are thinking dozens of conflicting thoughts a minute—and so when you are watching a fight in a film, there should be dozens of cuts per minute.[20] In

---

[20] This would make the audience participate emotionally in the fight itself. If, on the other hand, you wanted to create an objective distance—to have the audience observe the fight as a phenomenon in itself—then you would reduce the number of cuts considerably.

fact, statistically the two rates—of real-life blinking and of film cutting—are close enough for comparison: Depending on how it is staged, a convincing action sequence might have around twenty-five cuts a minute, whereas a dialogue scene would still feel "normal" (in an American film) averaging six cuts per minute or less.

You should be right with the blinks, perhaps leading them ever so slightly. I certainly don't expect the audience to blink at every cut—the cut point should be a *potential* blink point. In a sense, by cutting, by this sudden displacement of the visual field, you are blinking *for* the audience: You achieve the immediate juxtaposition of two concepts for them—what they achieve in the real world by blinking, as in Huston's example.

Your job is partly to anticipate, partly to control the thought processes of the audience. To give them what they want and/or what they need just before they have to "ask" for it—to be surprising yet self-evident at the same time. If you are too far behind or ahead of them, you create problems, but if you are right with them, leading them ever so slightly, the flow of events feels natural and exciting at the same time.

A Galaxy of Winking Dots

*A*long these lines, it would be fascinating to take an infrared film of an audience and find out when and in what patterns people blink when they are watching a movie. My hunch is that if an audience is really in the grip of a film, they are going to be thinking (and therefore blinking) with the rhythm of the film.

There is a wonderful effect that you can produce if you shine infrared light directly out in line with the lens of a camera. All animal eyes (including human eyes) will bounce a portion of that light directly back into the camera, and you will see bright glowing dots where the eyes are: It is a version of the "red-eye" effect in family snapshots taken with flashbulbs.

If you took a high-contrast infrared motion picture of an audience watching a film, placing the camera on stage and aligning the light source directly with the camera, you would see a galaxy of these dots against a field of black. And when someone in the audience blinked, you would see a momentary interruption in a pair of these dots.

If it were true, if there *were* times when those thousand dots winked more or less in unison, the film-maker would have an extremely powerful tool at his disposal. Coherent blinking would be a strong indication that the audience was thinking together, and that the film was working. But when the blinking became scattered, it would indicate that he may have lost his audience, that they had begun to think about where to go for dinner, or whether their car was parked in a safe place, etc.

When people are deeply "in" a film, you'll notice that nobody coughs at certain moments, even though they may have a cold. If the coughing were purely an autonomic response to smoke or congestion, it would be randomly constant, no matter what was happening on screen. But the audience holds back at certain moments, and I'm suggesting that blinking is something like coughing in this sense. There is a famous live recording of pianist Sviatoslav Richter playing Mussorgsky's *Pictures at an Exhibition* during a flu epidemic in Bulgaria many years ago. It is just as plain as day what's going on: While he was playing certain passages, no one coughed. At those moments, he was able to suppress, with his artistry, the coughing impulse of 1,500 sick people.

I think this subconscious attention to the blink is also something that you would probably find as a hidden factor in everyday life. One thing that may make you nervous about a particular person is that you feel, without knowing it, that his blinking is wrong. "He's blinking too much" or "He's not blinking enough" or "He's blinking at the wrong time." Which means he is not really listening to you, thinking along with you.

Whereas somebody who is really focused on what you are saying will blink at the "right" places at the "right" rate, and you will feel comfortable in this person's presence. I think we know these things intuitively, subconsciously, without having to be told, and I wouldn't be surprised to find that it is part of our built-in strategy for dealing with each other.

When we suggest that someone is a bad actor, we are certainly not saying that he is a bad human being; we are just saying that this person is not as fully *in* the character as he wants us to believe, and he's nervous about it. You can see this clearly in political campaigns, where there is sometimes a vivid distinction between who somebody is and who they want the voters to believe they are: Something will always be "wrong" with the rate and moment that these people blink.

That brings me back to one of the central responsibilities of the editor, which is to establish an interesting, coherent rhythm of emotion and thought—on the tiniest and the largest scales—that allows the audience to trust, to give themselves to the film. Without their knowing why, a poorly edited film will cause the audience to hold back, unconsciously saying to themselves, "There's something scattered and nervous about the way the film is thinking, the way it presents itself. I don't want to think that way; therefore, I'm not going to give as much of myself to the film as I might." Whereas a good film that is well-edited seems like an exciting extension and elaboration of the audience's own feelings and thoughts, and they will therefore give themselves to it, as it gives itself to them.

AFTER WORD

NON-LINEAR DIGITAL EDITING

The Unbearable Lightness

*I*n the first decades of this century, the film editor simply projected the uncut film, made notes, and then returned to a room equipped only with a bench, a pair of scissors, a magnifying glass, and the knowledge that the distance from the tip of his nose to the fingers of his outstretched arm represented about three seconds.[1] The cutting room was a kind of tailor shop in which time was the cloth. There was no other way to view the film except on a projector, so the editor patiently and somewhat intuitively stitched the fabric of his film together based on the impressions received in that first screening.

It is startling to recall that the humble Moviola— that frog-green fixture of every editing room over the

---

[1] At that time, film was generally projected at sixteen frames per second.

last seventy years—was initially rejected by these pioneering editors as expensive and cumbersome, even dangerous.[2] Still worse, its main feature—the ability to study the *motion* of the images before deciding which frame to cut on—was dismissed as a crutch that would simply get in the way of the work to be done.

So after an initial attempt to penetrate the industry, the Moviola was offered—implausibly—to the general public as a way of viewing home movies. It probably would have withered as a footnote to film history had not a fortuitous technical breakthrough occurred in 1927: sound.

Sound—The Talking Picture—was the Trojan horse that turned the situation around. No magnifying glass or three-second rule of thumb could help the editor lip-read those silent frames, so the now "double-headed" Moviola (picture and sound) was grudgingly wheeled through the studio gates, where it has been ever since.

Now the shoe is on the other foot, of course, and the beloved Moviola is shoring up the gates of "real" (i.e., mechanical) editing against the sophisticated assault of a number of electronic systems that have

---

[2] In those days, film was printed on explosive nitrate stock, and you did not thoughtlessly put it next to sources of heat (such as the lamp of a Moviola). Even being a projectionist was a life-threatening job: In some of the older theaters, you can still see the heavy "fail-safe" door that would close automatically in case there was a fire in the projection room. For similar reasons, the editor did not make the splices himself, since this involved heat, but only indicated *where* the splice was to be made. The actual assembly was done in another room safely down the hall, on a hot-splicer operated by a specialized technician.

emerged over the last decade or so: CMX, Montage, EditDroid, Avid, E-Pix, EMC, D-Vision, and Lightworks, as well as a number of others that have come and gone.

In fact, a tremendous amount of research and development has been invested in these systems, particularly when you consider that, although professional *film* is an expensive medium, there is not a lot of professional *film equipment* in the world, so there usually has not been much money to be made in improving it.

Television equipment, on the other hand, offers a world wide potential for profit at both the professional and the consumer levels, and the present wave of interest for improving post-production electronically comes in part from those who see a final merging of the two worlds of film and television, and hence a significant increase in the amount of money to be made.[3]

But electronic editing is not only being pushed by the hardware developers: Throughout the 1980s, a strong pull has also come from filmmakers such as George Lucas, Oliver Stone, Jim Cameron, Carroll Ballard, Bernardo Bertolucci, and Francis Coppola, all of whom have used electronic systems to edit their films. Lucas has gone as far as to become a developer himself with his EditDroid system. And short of actually creating marketable hardware, Francis Coppola has been one of the leading advocates and

---

[3] Avid, for instance, is delivering completely digital, non-tape TV news stations to Eastern Europe for around $1 million each.

users of electronic editing from the mid-1970s to the present.

What resistance remains, on the other hand, mostly comes from experienced feature editors who are comfortable with the well-worn peculiarities of the mechanical systems that have waged and won many creative battles for them, and who are reluctant to abandon them now for a system whose benefits have not been conclusively proven. Arguments are used that sound similar to those arrayed against the Moviola in the 1920s, but the difference this time is the grudging admission from everyone that something electronic is inevitable, although the timetable is open to question.

I would characterize my own experience with computerized editing as interested observer and occasional practitioner. My first encounter coincided with my introduction to Francis Coppola in 1968: He and George Lucas were investigating an early CMX system down the street from where I was working, and I came along to take a look.

The potential of what I saw naively made me think that this would overwhelm the industry in, at most, five years. So a couple of years later, after American Zoetrope had been launched in San Francisco, we prepared a proposal for using the CMX system to edit the first *Godfather* film, but nothing came of it: Storage and access were still too limited for the amount of footage generated by a feature film. Six years later, though, Francis installed a linear video-editing system on which he could experiment with different story structures for *Apocalypse Now,* and I used it to compose the series of overlapping four-element dissolves in the first reel of that film. Otherwise, *Apocalypse* was traditionally edited on two Moviolas (Richie Marks and Jerry Greenberg) and two KEM 8-plates (Lisa Fruchtman and myself).[4]

After *Apocalypse,* Francis and I didn't get the opportunity to work together again on a feature until *Godfather, Part III (1990),* and although I had started using a database for editorial record-keeping in 1982, I worked directly on film throughout the 1980s. Francis had continued to use some degree of video editing on all his films during this period, from *One From the Heart (1980)* to *Tucker (1988).* His "Silverfish"—a customized Airstream motorhome packed with electronic editing and monitoring equipment—first made its appearance on *One From the Heart.*

By the time of *Godfather, Part III,* however, he had moved from linear videotape systems up to the random-access, computer-controlled Montage editing system, and Lisa Fruchtman started using it in the fall of 1989 to put together the first cut of *Godfather, Part III.* Another Montage workstation was added when Barry Malkin joined the film in the spring of 1990, but when I came along a few months later in August, it just didn't seem practical—seeing that the film was due to come out in November—to add a third, so I worked directly on film. A few months later, I

---

[4] We did, however, mix the film's soundtrack on an automated MCI board—a process in some ways not unlike computerized editing.

did use the Montage to assemble the *Godfather Trilogy,* a ten-hour compilation of all three *Godfather* films; and two years later I used the Avid to together several music videos and to create a three-minute, five-level "newspaper" montage for the film *I Love Trouble* (1994).

Electronic editing systems are now being almost universally employed for commercials, television shows, and music videos, but their use on feature films presents a set of unique technical and creative problems that stem from the large—at times very large—amount of film that has to be manipulated and the need to translate accurately from 35mm to digital and back again.

So far, not all of the editors who have used computer-assisted systems have reported an unqualified success, at least logistically. In addition, even with recent breakthroughs, an electronic system may increase the budget of a film considerably over editing in film alone.[5] But most editors who have been exposed to them remain enthusiastic about the potential of these systems, and there is general agreement on the list of advertised features that enticed them into the electronic labyrinth in the first place—features which occasionally had a "will-o'-the-wisp" quality, dissolving just when they seemed within grasp.

- **Increased speed** is certainly the single most significant virtue of electronic systems, since speed appeal's to both the studios who want the film done quickly and to editors who are trying to

---

[5] An increase of from $100,000 to $300,000 if all the selected takes are printed on film as well as being digitized.

pack as much creativity as they can into every hour that the studio will give them. "How quickly can you do this?" is frequently the first question that will be asked of an editor, and any tool that can give a time advantage will be welcomed. The quickness of electronic systems comes about for many reasons, mostly through the instant random access to the material.

• *Reduced cost* for the workprint: For certain films this might be an option, since it is possible to digitize the image directly from the 35mm negative at roughly one-third the cost of making workprint. Once the images are edited, only the takes that were included in the cut need to be printed, which might reduce the film's workprint budget by ninety percent. (Some films may bypass the workprint stage entirely and cut the negative based on the system's Edit Decision List, but this has its risks.)

• *Fewer people* employed in the cutting room, since the computer automatically takes care of such things as filing trims, making lists, etc., that are usually handled by several assistants and apprentices.

• *Overall savings* would seem to arise naturally from the three previous items: If you can do your work faster, if you employ fewer people, and if you do not have to print all the selected takes, it seems that you should be able to reduce the budget accordingly. As we will see, this may not yet—practically speaking—be the case. But theoretically it is enticing.

- *Easier access* to the material. The traditional editing room has a certain medieval "guild" feel to it, with a well-defined hierarchy and long apprenticeships spent in coding and reconstituting—crafts that are non-existent in the digital domain. Simply stated, here is the goal of electronic editing: If you can operate a word processor, you can edit a film on one of these systems. This is a goal, not yet a reality, but there are many directors who would not think of touching a Moviola who do not hesitate to use an electronic system.

- *A more civilized working environment* free from the noise and the "physicality" of the Moviola (even the more modern KEM) and film itself. The electronic image you are looking at does not get scratched, torn, burned, and is not even physically spliced the way film is. You can see what you are doing more calmly and clearly.

- *Preservation of different versions* of the film. Just as there are no trims to worry about, electronic editing also keeps every version of a scene filed for future reference. By comparison, in conventional editing, there is no "going back" unless you make the deliberate (and time-consuming) decision to make a separate copy of the scene onto duplicating film or video. Along those same lines, electronic systems offer you the possibility of looking at a shot the way it was before it was cut into the film.

- *Satellite transmission:* Once an image is digitized, it then becomes possible to transmit it instantly from one part of the world to another, like cinematic faxes, via satellite. A producer in Los Angeles, for instance, can see digital dailies for a film on location in Paris, with no delay for shipping or customs. The material can then be edited in Los Angeles and sent back via satellite to the director in Paris.

• ***Integration with electronic special effects:*** For the same reasons, the electronic systems make it convenient to send material back and forth from the editing room to the special-effects house, where increasingly sophisticated electronic special effects can be applied to the film and then sent back to the editor. Traditional fades, dissolves, and wipes can be evaluated instantly, sets can be "topped" with photographs of real locations, crowds can be cloned and made to look five times as numerous. But this is just the tip of the electronic iceberg.

Despite all these alleged advantages, however, the Moviola is still with us, and we find ourselves somehow stuck in a lingering electro-mechanical "transition phase"—one that has lasted two decades longer than I would have guessed when I first looked at the CMX system in 1968. After all, 2001 is only a few years away, the 33⅓ LP is history, word processors have universally replaced typewriters . . . and yet here we are, still listening to the clattering of the Moviola, with scratched film all over the floor, splicers, tape, trim bins, grease pencils, etc., etc. It is the awareness of this odd technological lag that is one of the stronger undercurrents pushing electronic editing forward: simply the feeling that somehow . . . *shouldn't we be getting along?* It certainly doesn't arise from the fact that the Moviola can't do the job, and do it well, on some of the most "modern" films produced today, but it just doesn't seem "right" to be using nineteenth-century technologies on the eve of the twenty-first. In one sense, the persistence of the Moviola is about as surprising as it would be seeing an old manual Underwood being loaded onto the Space Shuttle.

What is going on?

Simply stated, some of the non-linear systems were oversold. And some of the "defects" of the traditional mechanical systems are not all that bad after all; in fact, there is a considerable amount of concealed wisdom in film, particularly when the whole editorial process, from beginning to end, is taken into consideration. By the same token, the four-stroke automobile engine may not be theoretically the most ideal, but in the real world it has been fine-tuned by decades of experience, every aspect of it has been fully studied and taken advantage of, and plenty of standardized parts are available if anything goes wrong.

What would resolve the ambivalence of this "transition phase" in a single stroke, of course, is the 1990's equivalent of *sound:* some new "Trojan horse" that would transform the industry, tipping the balance irrevocably in favor of electronics. Until that day, though (and it may arrive tomorrow), we should probably resign ourselves to this ambivalence the way turn-of-the-century householders learned to live with the shortcomings of those gas/electric chandeliers that were the temporary, practical compromise between efficient (but expensive and unreliable) electricity and dependable (but dangerous and inefficient) gas.

Some of the shortcomings of the digital systems are, similarly, *teething problems*—temporary awkwardness like the gas/electric chandelier that will shortly be ironed out. In the meantime, they can be annoying and even, at times, catastrophic, but they are not fundamental defects.

Another group of problems is apparently more deeply ingrained. These *systemic problems* are moderately disturbing since it is not clear what can be done about them: Their solution would involve fundamental modifications either to the systems themselves or to the interface between the system and the "outside" world.

And a third group of problems are more perplexing still, not because they are necessarily harder to solve than the previous two, but because they are partly *retreats* masquerading as *advances,* and so it is hard to see them as problems in the first place. For the most part, though, these *creative problems* have solutions that are fairly straightforward once they have been uncovered.

Teething Problems

- *Insufficient memory:* The normal feature film generates about forty to fifty hours of raw material, so to have all this available to the editor at any time requires a formidable amount of hard-disc storage. A rough rule of thumb is that it takes one gigabyte (one billion bytes of information) to store a half-hour of adequately detailed video image. So the average feature film, with forty hours of workprint, would need 40 x 2 = 80 billion bytes of digital storage. *Apocalypse Now,* however, had 230 hours (236 miles!) of workprint, which represents 460 gigabytes (460,000,000,000 bytes) of storage at current rates of compression. In the old days (i.e., five years ago—and five years is a computer "generation"), this was an impractical amount of memory. Now, memory towers of sixty gigabytes each cost in the neighborhood of $20,000, so a film like *Apocalypse Now* could be accommodated by installing eight towers (480 gigabytes) for a purchase price of $160,000.

When memory was not so cheap, "workarounds" had to be found to deal with this problem. Five years ago, the average best available (i.e., practical) storage was eight gigabytes, or four hours of film available to the editor at any one time. As a result of this, the storage for the average feature film (forty hours of workprint) had to be broken down into a least ten sections, or "loads," which made it inconvenient to cross over from one part of the film to another. This was awkward to say the least, and it undercut many of the advantages gained in other areas.

In traditional film editing, *all* of the workprint—no matter how much there is—is equally accessible to the editor at any moment. It may take longer to retrieve than it would with a computerized system, but there has always been a liberating sense that you could cut from anything to anything else and it wouldn't make any difference in the bookkeeping. After many frustrating years, this is now finally true for electronic editing, and the solution to the storage problem is without a doubt one of the main factors creating the surge of interest in digital systems within the last few years.

• ***Actual ease of making the cut itself:*** Some of the systems have been overly keyboard-intensive, which is not what most film editors are (or should be) comfortable with: There needs to be an easy and immediate kinetic feedback between the material and the eye-hand coordination of the editor, both in terms of selecting the desired frame and making the "splice" itself. Editing is a kind of "frozen dance," and this depends on engaging as much of the editor's body as possible.

Digital buffers offer the most promising solution to this kind of problem, especially if they are combined with interface hardware that mimics the physical engagement automatically offered by the mechanical devices—the satisfying feeling of using the Moviola's brake, for instance, to stop instantly on a desired frame, and then the ability to creep forward and backward frame by frame by rotating a flywheel, without digital artifacts in the sound.

In years to come, I expect that editors will find the "physical interface" that pleases them best, and they will be able to take it around from job to job, as radio announcers do with their favorite microphones.

- ***"Works best when needed least":*** Frequently, when called upon to perform a series of fast picture cuts and complicated sound edits, some of these systems will tell you in one way or another that you have overloaded their processing ability, and they can no longer show you your work in real-time. This is simply a question of adding enough memory and processing ability to do the job. But memory equals money, so as the cost of memory drops, the ability of these machines will rise.

- ***Low resolution on the monitor scree:.*** The lower the screen resolution, the greater the eye-strain and the less efficiently the editor works. In addition, lack of screen resolution will unconsciously encourage the editor to use close-ups, which may not be the correct artistic decision for a feature film shown in 35mm. The determining factor for selecting a particular shot is frequently, "Can you register the expression in the actor's eyes?" If you can't, you (the editor) will tend to use the next closer shot, even though the wider shot may be more than adequate when seen on the big screen. This, of course, affects the creative flow of the film.

If you are cutting on film, you are also frequently looking at the film in widescreen projection, which further "educates" your eye about what is actually present in the shot. If you are only looking at video, you are denied this unless the screen is very sharp—sharper than broadcast video is at present. Hence the need in electronic systems to conform the workprint and "pull it along" after you as you make changes.

There is also a direct ratio between image quality and storage time. Broadcast quality (Avid AVR 27) is available but requires an unrealistic one gigabyte for every seven minutes of time. At this rate, even a modest feature film would require 350 gigabytes (six towers) of storage. And remember, 35mm film is at least four times sharper than broadcast-quality video. As a practical compromise, editors seem to be settling for AVR 5 or 5e, which runs about twenty-five minutes per gigabyte. Resolution of the image at this rating is good, but the backgrounds of detailed long shots tend to break up into impressionistic square blocks of pure color.

Ultimately, this can be solved by larger and cheaper memory banks and even more efficient ways of compressing and storing visual material.

- **Bottlenecks:** Because of the high rental/purchase costs of computer-assisted systems compared to Moviolas or KEMs, the number of machines per film has to be limited, and this has the potential to create scheduling bottlenecks. If Moviolas or KEMs are being used, however, it is easy to hire another editor to work on the film, or to have assistants cutting under supervision, in order to meet a deadline.

A "generation" ago (five years!), each electronic system was a self-contained entity, and bookkeeping had to be done after the editor had gone home, which meant a night shift for the first assistant with consequent lack of contact between the editor and his main collaborator in the process. Now, with multiple workstations accessing the same memory banks, not only can assistants log material while the editor is working, but other complete workstations can be piggybacked on and two editors can work simultaneously, even on the same material.

• *Half-frame problem:* In the U.S., film runs at twenty-four frames per second and video runs at thirty frames, so there is a mathematical "five video frames for every four film frames" compatibility (known as "3-2 pulldown") that has to be worked out if the two systems are going to mesh. As of 1995, this has largely been solved, but it was a surprisingly persistent problem for the analog electronic systems (Montage, EditDroid). What it boiled down to was this: There are times in electronic editing when you have selected a video frame that has no numerical equivalent in film, so the computer has to make an arbitrary decision about which "side" of this phantom frame the edit should be. If there was only one version of the film ever made, this would be easier to resolve, but in fact there are changes made upon changes made upon changes, so a decision to come down on the "left" side of a particular cut for the first version of the film may be followed by a decision to come down on the "right" side of the same cut for the second, and errors of these "phantom frames" can be compounded.

With the digital systems (Avid, Lightworks, D-vision) the half-frame problem is gone because they work in a true 24fps environment. However, a subtler problem still lurks: 29.97fps.

Systemic Problems

The second group of problems are more intractable than the first. Even when they have been identified, it is not immediately clear what can be done. Most of them relate to the difficulties encountered in dealing with the conformation between film and digital material and back again.

• ***29.97 frames per second:*** I just said that video runs at thirty frames per second, but it doesn't, actually. In the United States—for reasons that are primarily of historical interest—color video runs at 29.97 frames per second, in order to insure compatibility with old black-and-white sets. This is a potential problem for twenty-four-frame digital systems because film negative is frequently transferred to analog video at the lab, and then the image is digitized from that tape into the editing machine by the editors. This process not only requires the "2-3 pulldown" mentioned above, generating those phantom frames, but what could be called a "29.97 pulldown," effectively slowing the frame rate by .1% (the sound is slowed by the same amount). As a result, the discrete twenty-four-to-twenty-four process is infected with a .1% margin of error on input. Furthermore, the output of Avid or Lightworks for screening purposes (and for sound editors) is again video at 29.97fps, where those errors can be accumulated or compounded.

The practical result of this electronic rat's nest is that when a sound editor comes to place an effect in sync with the video picture he has been given, there is a corrosive doubt that what he does at this point will not correspond with what he finds when he gets on the mixing stage, where true 24fps film is running through the projector.

A few labs can digitize the image directly to disc from the negative, giving a true twenty-four-to-twenty-four correspondence. This should become the standard in years to come, but bottlenecks presently limit access to a potentially ideal solution. A videotape of the dailies can be made simultaneously with the negative/ digital transfer, but this should be for reference and backup only, not as a means of subsequently transferring to digital.

Everything is much simpler in most of Europe, where both film and video run at a solid

25fps, which is exactly half of the frequency rate (50hz) of their mains power.

• **Sync problem:** If the master videotape (or digitized disc) for these systems is made directly off the film negative, the soundtrack then has to be "spun" in, in sync, from the original recording, and this is an as-yet imperfect science, dependent on the skill and professionalism of the person doing it. If there is a problem, it is extremely important to catch it before the video is retransferred to disc, since it is almost impossible—practically speaking—to put the genie of sync back in his bottle once he has escaped: There will always be a lingering doubt that something is not right. The reason for this is that there is, as yet, no digital equivalent of film's ironclad sprocket/code-number relationship, which is the universally accepted standard in 35mm sound work.

• **The dialogue track:** The emphasis in video editing has been primarily on picture, with the assumption that the dialogue track follows along without much complication. In fact, film editing in 35mm frequently involves some sophisticated dialogue cutting, with resolution down to 1/96th of a second (a cut can be made wherever there is a sprocket, and there are ninety-six sprockets in a second's worth of film). As yet, none of the electronic *image* editing systems are capable of this precision in *sound*—their level of resolution is the same as for picture: the single frame, or 1/24th of a second.

This limitation passes along an ambiguity to the sound editor who receives the picture editor's work: Were these specific sound edits what the picture editor actually intended, or are they just the result of the crudeness of the tools? In theory, digital systems should be able to give editorial resolution down to the width of the highest reproducible frequency, which is to say 1/20,000 of a second.

• *Sound conformation:* With the increase in audio quality of the sound of the digital machines, it has become convenient to mix together and then output all the editor's temporary work tracks (dialogue, music, sound effects) onto film and to project this in sync with the 35mm workprint. This is advantageous for screening purposes, but only useful to the sound editors as an indication of the picture editor's intentions. Until the "universal file format" exists to permit the sound editor to access the film's digital tracks directly, there is no easy way to "copy" the work the picture editor has done on the soundtrack—consequently, it all needs to be recut from original elements and reassembled using the temporary mix as a guide.

There needs to be an output, or printout, of all the editor's dialogue tracks, with cutting accuracy at least to 1/96th of a second (sprocket accuracy). It is not that it can't be done, theoretically, but the solutions offered by the electronic systems thus far have been largely inadequate compared to what happens naturally in the course of editing film itself.

- **Lag from approved version to screening.**
  When you feel that you have "got" the version
  you want on video, there will be a delay of a
  few days before you can see it projected in
  35mm, due to the process of conforming the
  workprint to the shot list. A rough rule of thumb
  here is that it takes about a day per reel to do
  the original conformation, and a little under an
  hour per reel to conform the subsequent
  changes.

  This delay is acceptable at the early stages,
  but it becomes more annoying and awkward
  the closer you get to finishing the film—particularly at the point that you are previewing
  before an audience. The tendency then becomes
  almost irresistible to make the changes in between previews directly on film to minimize the
  turnaround time.

- **"Reverse cut":** If you do make changes directly
  on film, the question becomes, "Do you con-
  tinue to conform the electronic shot list to what
  you have done on film ('reverse cutting'), or do
  you let go and simply make the transition to
  film complete?" If you do, this means that you
  have to be geared up technically to cutting to-
  tally on film, which may beg the question of
  why you cut electronically in the first place.

- **Crew stratification:** Conforming the workprint
  requires assistants who will tend to become
  divorced from the creative process of editing—
  they become "negative" cutters assembling a
  workprint from lists of computer-generated num-

bers. There is the potential for an "us" and "them" mentality to take hold because the people working on film are often physically as well as emotionally separated from the electronic editing.[6]

Traditional film editing generally is (at least, it should be!) a close-in activity in which all the members of the crew feel that they are part of the process. This automatically brings with it the benefits of involvement and—in the longer term—training of potential editors who are already familiar with the creative give-and-take of the editing room.

• *Increased cost:* As I indicated earlier, if you are editing electronically *and* all the selected takes are printed as workprint (and all sound transfers done to 35mm mag and synched up and coded in order to show to the studio executives, stars, etc.), the total digital/analog editorial budget of a film can be more expensive than analog film alone: at this point, in the range of $100,000 to $300,000.

To pay for this extra cost, post-production executives at the studios will expect editors who are using the electronic systems to finish two months earlier than if they were editing on film alone. This puts obvious strains on the creative process.

Most of these systemic problems will go away on

---

[6] Some film services are now offering to conform the 35mm as a subcontracted job, like negative cutting, so that it is truly physically separate from the editorial process.

the day that 35mm film is no longer shown theatrically—when moving pictures are shown on some sort of luminous, large-format, liquid-crystal screen, and film itself is relegated to the production phase only, if that. Then, editing will proceed directly—perhaps automatically—from an electronic shot list to the final "on line" assembly of images, both for previewing and, after any revisions, the electronic "answer print."

But as long as 35mm film is shown theatrically, it is going to need to be previewed theatrically; and as long as 35mm film is previewed theatrically, 35mm film must be printed and conformed. This means that if you are using an electronic system, the editorial department must "carry" the workprint along, bringing it up to date with each revision to the electronic master. And this means that at some point you must gear up, both in terms of equipment and personnel, to a level that is almost as complete as if you were cutting in film alone.

Creative Problems

Finally, some of the very qualities that are used to promote computerized editing—speed, fewer assistants, reduced bookkeeping, easier access—have a shadowy flip side where these advantages are questionable. It is interesting to look at things from this "upside-down" perspective—not only because of what may be learned in the process, but because computerized editing is still at a stage where it is flexible enough to incorporate

*some of the hidden advantages of mechanical editing.
I say "hidden" because in a number of cases these
qualities are the very "defects" that computerized editing is designed to improve or eliminate.*

- **Speed:** Computerized editing systems achieve
  most of their speed through random-access—
  being able to retrieve the requested material in-
  stantaneously. This allows the editor to do many
  things, such as instantly compare line-readings
  from different takes. But the speed of random-
  access systems ultimately depends on specific
  instructions: The clearer you are about what you
  want, the faster they are. You, in turn, are more
  dependent on the quality and quantity of your
  initial notes and opinions. As the film evolves,
  however, its needs change and those initial opinions may become outdated: A shot that was initially considered useless may, in a different context, become useful. Unless there is a way of
  constantly re-examining the material, some of
  it may remain buried forever under the enigmatic epitaph "No Good." The greater the
  amount of material, the more true this is.

  On the other hand, linear systems (such as
  the KEM) store the film in ten-minute rolls, and
  therefore require you to scan through related
  material in your search for what you *want.* Frequently—invariably in my experience—you find
  what you need instead: some shot that captures
  a moment better than the one you were after,
  but which you could not have described in

advance of seeing it. You also get to know the material better, because you are constantly browsing through it, looking for different things, in different states of mind.

So the real issue is not just how fast you can go, but where are you going? It doesn't help to arrive quickly if you wind up in the wrong place. And if the destination involves a complete knowledge of the material and using that material to the fullest, in the most flexible way, the linear systems may have an edge, despite being "slower" at certain things such as retrieval of a specific shot.

In fact, there is no reason that a degree of linearity cannot be introduced into electronic systems through software commands, or simply by making a practice of "scanning through" all the dailies of a scene, but the first step is to recognize that there is this hidden serendipity to linear systems. Random-access is such a good selling point—it is technically "sexy" and satisfying to demonstrate—that it is difficult to realize that it may have its limitations creatively.[7] It is even more difficult for designers to add back the very thing—linearity—that they were proudest of eliminating.

Also, a certain amount of "mulling" can occur spontaneously with mechanical systems:

---

[7] Word processors, for the same reasons, facilitate changes but discourage rewriting. It is so easy to change a single word that first drafts tend to be patched up rather than rewritten, and the quality of the writing suffers.

Because they require a necessary amount of busy-work, this is a time when the hands can be engaged automatically and the mind is allowed to think more subconsciously about the work. If you are always working "on line" at an expensive workstation, the pressure is on every decision to count, and your decisions may become overly conscious—particularly since random-access requires you to articulate every request.

But, ultimately, technology is hardly ever the determining factor in questions of speed vs. creativity—here, we are in the domain of the human spirit. Balzac, 180 years ago, wrote eighty classic novels in twenty years, using just a quill pen. Who among our word-processors today can even approach such a record? In the 1930s, Jean Renoir made a commercially successful feature film (*On purge Bébé*) in three weeks—from concept to finished product. And early in his career, Kurosawa—directing and editing himself—would have the first cut of his films done two days after shooting.

However, if you are selling one of these machines, it is logical to emphasize speed because pure speed is what interests the people who are paying hundreds of thousands of dollars for the equipment you are trying to sell. But instead of "speed" it would actually be more honest to advertise "increased options"—the new system will allow the work to remain flexible longer, which is to say, the moment of decisive commitment can be delayed. In the 1930s, you had to plan out very carefully in advance where you were going to put the camera when the Technicolor three-strip blimp weighed half a ton. With lightweight cameras, fast film, and DAT recorders, you can change your mind up to the last instant, and even beyond. Does it all happen faster? Not necessarily: A level of complexity is frequently added that eats up all the time gained. Is it better? That is arguable. The year 1939 is still recognized by many as the high-water mark of the American film industry.

• **Sync:** The electronic systems ensure that the sound and picture are always in sync, whereas with the mechanical systems, the editor has to pay constant attention to the relationship of code numbers. This is another feature that the electronic systems would claim gives greater speed—freeing the editor from any concern about sync.

But, in fact, a surprisingly small proportion of the dialogue in a feature film is synched with its original picture—probably considerably less than half. Overlaps, point-of-view shots, special effects, stunt shots, replacements of line readings, etc., require the editor to supply a different sound than the original sync track. So there is just as strong a premium on sliding and replacing sound as there is on it being in sync in the first place, and here the electronic systems can become cumbersome, not only in the initial slipping or replacement of track but in the organization and output of shot lists for conformation purposes. The mechanical systems, by contrast, don't "care" whether the material is in sync or not, so it is all the same, operationally.

I should mention that my own preference is to cut without sound wherever possible—even for dialogue scenes—initially supplying the sound from my memory and imagination, and only adding sound at a later stage in the process. As a result, I am less tied to the actuality and hopefully more apt to discover interesting juxtapositions of sound and image. Again, it is not that the electronic systems can't achieve the same thing, but because "sync" has been isolated as a virtue, the systems tend to encourage that and discourage other, perhaps more creative, paths to the use of sound.

• ***Fewer assistants:*** This may be achieved some day, but films that have used non-linear digital editing have in practice required *more* assistants than usual, because there have to be *people* to handle the conforming of the 35mm workprint as well as helping with the logging and database work required. As I mentioned earlier, this kind of crew tends to stratify along film/video lines and produce a subtle alienation that is not ultimately good for the film or the industry as a whole.

Arguably, the greatest period of creativity in painting occurred at a time—three to five hundred years ago—when painters required assistants to prepare the pigments and canvasses.

All of the great painters of the Renaissance started out as assistants to established artists—there were no art schools as such—and moved up the ladder, starting to help with the actual painting at a certain stage, until they were ready to work on their own, with their own assistants.

Not only did this provide on-site training, free from the fog of theory that can settle over academic situations, but I am sure that the presence of other people during the act of creation kept painting grounded in a way that it is obviously not today, when it is done almost exclusively in isolation. I cannot count the number of times that feedback from my assistants has kept me "honest" about what worked or didn't work: They are my first audience, so to speak. And how many times they have provided the film with ideas beyond what I could have thought up myself.

The ultimate aim of computerized editing, however, is "one man/one machine"—an editor working as a painter works, alone in a room with all the material at his fingertips and no need of anyone around to help. If this is ever achieved technically, it will be interesting to see the films that result, and to discover whether the collaboration that is the essence of filmmaking is not in some way compromised by this technical "advance."

- **_Reduced bookkeeping:_** This is an area where computers shine above all—the record-keeping abilities of the electronic systems are impressive—but even here there is a cautionary note. First of all, it is not necessary to have a fully computer-driven system to gain many of the advantages that a computer can bring to the editing room: A PC or Macintosh with a relational database can be bought for $3,000 to $5,000 (or rented) and can do away with most of the repetitious work—log books, code books, etc.— that is still done by hand in many editing rooms.

Unquestionably, electronic systems gain a significant advantage by eliminating the filing of trims—something that on an average feature can become the full-time occupation of at least one assistant. Another related advantage is the ability to memorize different versions of scenes for future reference. This, however, is a slightly more dubious asset: It can open up a "sorcerer's apprentice" proliferation of help that may ultimately overwhelm the very people it is trying to assist.

Editing is (or should be) progressive—you are moving forward all the time. Even if you go back to a previous structure, it will not be (or should not be) exactly as it was, but reflect in subtle ways what has happened to the film as a whole since the scene was first put together. But by keeping every version of a scene, you can easily drown in all the variations, feeling some obligation to look at each of them and incorporate a little of each in subsequent versions. The result is that you may lose time in unproductive discussion and produce work that can have a "stitched-together," Frankenstein kind of feel, rather than being organically whole and alive.

At any rate, if you are cutting on film and different versions of a scene need to be saved, it can also be done inexpensively simply by making a videotape (or reversal film dupe). That is usually all that is needed—some reference point that can trigger new ideas. At any rate, even here the motto should be "the fewer the better."

• *No rewinding:* With random-access systems there is no delay in going back to the head of a sequence once you have arrived at the end, like jumping from one section of a CD to another. This is another time-saving aspect that has a "shadow" side: electronic systems find it difficult to show the assembly of edits in any other form than normal-speed forward—they try, but it is the visual equivalent of scanning audio in a CD—brief sections are excerpted, like skipping a flat stone across the surface of a lake.

Since normal-speed forward is the way the film is going to be seen by an audience, why would there be a need to see it any other way? For the same reason that painters will frequently look at their work in a mirror upside down: By inverting the image, it is momentarily freed of content and can be looked at as pure structure. Driven by identical impulses, Catalonian architect Antonio Gaudí used to build the models for his structures upside down, hanging them by wires so that he could immediately see the effect of an imbalance.

In the course of assembling a sequence on the KEM, I will frequently fast-rewind through the picture head, and there is something in the pure alternation of shapes and colors, seen out of the corner of my eye at high-speed reverse, that tells me something about the structure of the piece that I could not learn by looking at it "straight on" at normal-speed forward.

This is a hidden value of mechanical, linear editing that the designers of the electronic systems probably eliminated without even being aware that they were doing so, but there may be a way it could be reintroduced as an option once its values were recognized.

• ***Easier access:*** On the face of it, this should be a good thing, and it partakes of the general drift of technological innovation over the last thirty years. Consumers of electronic hardware can now purchase devices that were closely guarded professional secrets as little as ten years ago. This has been particularly true in sound: The average car-stereo system of today produces better sound than the most advanced re-recording studio of thirty years ago. It is not too hard to imagine that, a few years down the road, consumers will have editorial systems for their home videos that would make professionals envious today. And so they will, if the current trends of digital compression, manipulation, and storage keep accelerating at the same rate that they have over the last ten years.

The hard truth, though, is that easier access does not automatically make for better results. The accompanying sense that "anyone can do it" can easily result in a broth spoiled by too many cooks. All of us today are able to walk into an art store and buy—inexpensively—pigments and supplies that the Renaissance painters would have paid fortunes for. And yet, how many of us paint on their level today?

The slight reflective intake of breath that occurs when you find yourself engaged in a craft that is not available to the general public makes you take things a degree more seriously. In the correct dosage, this is not a bad thing: It is a sort of wake-up call to your higher instincts.

• *A more civilized working environment:* Many years ago, I remember seeing an advertisement in the *New Yorker* for an interior-decorating firm that showed a split-level Park Avenue apartment featuring a beautiful Steinway Grand placed in the foreground, and the text underneath asked us to "think of the music that Beethoven could have written if he had lived here!"

The physicality of the Moviola would have probably repelled the designers of that ad, and they would certainly have applauded the look of the computer-editing suite in comparison. But is physicality really a bad thing? What kind of music *would* Beethoven have written in that

apartment? And what would those interior deco-
rators have thought of Rodin's sculpture studio?
The most that can be said of the creative working environment is that it is probably a question of balance, like many things: comfortable,
but not too comfortable; organized, but not too
organized.

The editing room of a film can be a place
of considerable tension, and one of the "hidden" virtues of the mechanical systems is that
their very physicality requires you to move
around a lot—certainly in comparison to working on a computer in front of a video screen—
and this can serve as a means of releasing that
tension.

Although the flatbed systems are more physical than the computer, they require less physical movement than the Moviola, and when I
first started using a Steenbeck in 1969, after
having worked on the Moviola, I developed
what I called "Steenbeck Neck"—a tension in
the upper shoulders that came from sitting at
the Steenbeck and only having to move my fingers and wrists to edit. To combat this, I now
have my KEM raised fifteen inches off the
ground so that I work at it standing up, as I did
at the Moviola. This engages more of the body
in the process of cutting and is more comfortable in the long run. I would recommend it to
any editor suffering from neck/shoulder pain,
and would particularly recommend it as an
option for the electronic systems.

• ***Digital special effects:*** If anything has the potential to become the "Trojan horse" of the 1990's, it is this. Digital effects are now the industry standard and have increasingly replaced the traditional "optical" during the last five years: from the early "Harry" system that was used on *Ghost* through the Digital Image Manipulation that produced the T-2000 in *Terminator 2* and the dinosaurs in *Jurassic Park.* Their value is twofold: They can create images impossible to achieve by the usual photographic methods; and, although there are exceptions, they are generally less expensive and quicker than their photographic equivalents.

It is not clear what shape this will all take, but if it becomes significantly easier to move back and forth from editing to special effects, with no clear boundary between the two, and if there is a significant reduction in the cost and time to produce acceptable special effects, film may find itself the odd man out.

When regulated postal service was finally established in Great Britain and Royal mail started to be carried on trains for the first time—somewhere around 1840— it unleashed a torrent of letter-writing among those who were able to do so. People routinely dashed off twenty-page letters three times a week to several correspondents simultaneously, not so much because they had anything particularly compelling to say to each other, but simply from the exhilaration of being able to say it—and have it reliably received across the country in a matter of days, rather than the unreliable weeks or months that it took in the days of coach and horses.

We have something similar happening today with the fax machine and the Internet, but, in fact, any significant technological breakthrough will create a surge of exploratory interest that can only be satisfied by creating a pretext for the exploration. For a while, *what* is communicated is less important than the *means by which* it is communicated.[8] Eventually, the new technology is assimilated and content re-establishes itself. We are somewhere along that road with computer-assisted editing, but since things are still evolving so rapidly, it is hard to say exactly how far we have gone.

In the three years since the Australian publication of this book, several corners have been turned in electronic editing. What was then still a chaotic situation, with many systems competing for a limited market, has begun to sort itself out, with two digital companies—Avid and Lightworks—emerging as the General Motors and Ford of the non-linear world. It is now increasingly rare to find someone editing a feature directly on film, whereas three years ago this was not the case, and technical breakthroughs are continuing to occur on a regular basis so that the comparison with the state of the automotive industry of the 1920s is not far off. Not to mention that the price of "gasoline" (i.e., memory) is dropping twenty percent every three months.

---

[8] Viz. Marshall McLuhan's famous dictum: The Medium is the Message.

When I originally wrote this Afterword, I felt that we would not begin to emerge out of the digital/mechanical twilight zone—the "gas/electric chandelier" mode—until three milestones had been passed:

1) Memory storage becomes more efficient by an order of magnitude, so that it is possible to store at least forty to one hundred hours of high-quality picture "on line," having it all equally accessible at all times.

2) The cost of a fully operational system capable of editing a feature drops well below $100,000, or into the range that you would expect to spend for a KEM.

3) Film—as film—is no longer shown theatrically. Release prints are replaced by an electronic equivalent that is as good or better than 35mm film.

In fact or in practice, two of these milestones have now been passed. Reasonably priced sixty-gigabyte memory "towers" are available that hold thirty hours of adequately detailed digital image.[9] And a system with two full editorial workstations and an assistant station costs in the neighborhood of $250,000 (or just over $80,000 each), which begins to put it in the range of the increasingly obsolete KEM.

Today, I would add a fourth milestone:

4) The creation of the digital equivalent of the 35mm *sprocket/code* relationship: A

---

[9] Cost is around $20,000 per tower.

universal standard that would operate across all the technical environments in which image and sound are manipulated, and which would provide an immutable point of reference for any questions about the picture/sound/negative relationship.

Despite its many antiquated features, film still has this considerable advantage over the digital systems: An editor can move with great freedom from Moviola to KEM to Steenbeck to Editing Bench to Mix Theater to Screening Room, with stops off at the Lab and the Negative Cutter—all are unified by the "standard gauge" of the 35mm sprockets. This has yet to be achieved in the Digital Domain.

And we still have not achieved milestone number three—the abolition of film. As someone who grew up professionally with the clatter of the Moviola in his ears—but who is typing these words on a computer—I must say that I feel a mixture of anticipation, nostalgia, and regret even contemplating this one. Kodak is apparently two to ten years away from working prototypes of the Digital Theater. The cost of a projector in one of these installations would be in the neighborhood of $250,000, and the storage requirements would be 5,000 to 8,000 gigabytes per feature.

My own tendency, as early as that first encounter with the CMX in 1968, was an enthusiastic but naive acceptance of electronics in the editing room—it seemed natural and inevitable to me then and, on a certain level, it does now. On the other hand, my actual experience as an editor over the last thirty years has taken me over all of the mechanical backroads and thereby taught me a respect for much of the inherent (and some of the unwitting) wisdom of mechanical editing, which has been slowly accumulated through many tens of thousands of man-years of practical experience by the editing community.

Beyond the pros and cons, costs and schedules, though—and buried somewhere in thoughts about film's "tactility" and "feel"—is the plain fact of film's physical existence—that the image is actually captured, chemically, on celluloid. What we are communicating through film is so unsubstantial—fleeting emotions patterned with beams of colored light and waves of sound—that it is somehow restoratively balancing to be able to actually hold a frame of film in one's hand, light as it is. There is a wonderful alchemy in this: that hydrocarbons and silver and iron and various colored dyes, plus intangible time, can transmute themselves into the stuff of dreams.

But compared to the stream of a computer's weightless electrons and ghostly digits, film is gravity itself; and in our by-now-inevitable rush to embrace the electron's weightlessness for the intoxicating speed and flexibility it can give, let us see if we cannot use this lingering grace period to take another look at film's physicality and find a way to incorporate, somehow, various simulations of the best of that physicality into the new systems. A reel of film *is* obstinately the way it is and no other—unless you actually rearrange the matter out of which it is made—and there is an anchoring, inertial value in that which the fluttering electrons, for all their nervous power, do not share.

Walter Murch has been honored by both British and American Motion Picture Academies for his picture editing and sound mixing. In 1997, Murch received an unprecedented double Oscar for both film editing and sound mixing for *The English Patient* (1996, dir. A. Minghella), as well as the British Academy Award for best editing. Seventeen years earlier, he received an Oscar for best sound for *Apocalypse Now* (1979, dir. F. Coppola), as well as British and American Academy nominations for his picture editing on the same film. He also won a double British Academy Award for his film editing and sound mixing on *The Conversation* (1974, dir. F. Coppola), was nominated by both Academies for best film editing for *Julia* (1977, dir. F. Zinnemann), and received a double nomination from the American Academy in 1991 for best film editing for the films *Ghost* (dir. J. Zucker) and *The Godfather, Part III* (dir. F. Coppola).

Among Murch's recent credits are picture editing for *The Unbearable Lightness of Being* (1988, dir. P. Kaufman), *House of Cards* (1993, dir. M. Lessac), *Romeo is Bleeding* (1994, dir. P. Medak), and *First Knight* (1995, dir. J. Zucker). He was the re-recording mixer for *The Rainpeople* (1969, dir. F. Coppola), *THX-1138* (1971, dir. G. Lucas), *The Godfather* (1972, dir. F. Coppola), *American Graffiti* (1973, dir. G. Lucas), *The Godfather, Part II* (1974, dir. F. Coppola), and *Crumb* (1995, dir. T. Zweigoff), as well as all recent films for which he has also been picture editor. Screenplays on which he has collaborated include *THX-1138* and *The Black Stallion* (1979, dir. C. Ballard). Murch also directed and co-wrote the film *Return to Oz*, released by Disney in 1985.